Inspirational Baseball Stories for Kids 9-12

30 Legendary Tales from Baseball History for Beginning Readers

Ty McDaniel

Disclaimer

Without the publisher's prior written consent, no portion of this publication may be reproduced, stored in a retrieval system, or transmitted in any form or by any means, electronic, mechanical, photocopying, recording, scanning, or otherwise, except as permitted under Sections 107 or 108 of the United States Copyright Act of 1976. Although every precaution has been taken in preparing this book, the publisher is not liable for any mistakes, omissions, or damages resulting from the use of the material included within. This book is intended solely for entertainment and educational purposes. The opinions presented are those of the author alone and should not be construed as professional advice or directives. The reader's activities are his or her own responsibility. The author and publisher take no responsibility or liability for the purchaser or reader of these contents. The reader is responsible for his or her own usage of any products or techniques referenced in this publication.

Inspirational Baseball Stories for Kids 9-12
First Edition: July 26, 2023
Copyright © 2023 Caliber Brands Inc.

Contents

Introduction

Welcome to the thrilling world of baseball, where dreams become reality and victories become legend! This book will lead you on an exhilarating journey into the incredible stories of baseball players who have experienced triumphs that inspire us to excel in our own pursuits. Prepare to be encouraged, motivated, and lifted with a deeper appreciation for the game as we delve into these true stories that contain underlying teachings to overcome any obstacle in life.

Baseball is more than just a sport—it's a metaphor for life. Through the accounts of these extraordinary athletes, we will witness the immense power of determination, tenacity, teamwork, and the pursuit of excellence. Each chapter of this book introduces a different player who overcame difficult obstacles and left an unforgettable impression on the game.

From the courageous pitcher who conquered a physical disability to become a strikeout king to the charismatic outfielder who defied all odds to lead his team to victory-- each player's journey will capture your heart and inspire you to strive for greater heights. These are not fictional characters; rather, they are real individuals whose unwavering dedication and unyielding spirit have inspired millions.

In this book, you'll see how these remarkable athletes turned struggle into victory and setbacks into growth. Their stories will inspire you to believe in yourself, work hard, and never give up on reaching greatness.

This book was written for you if you are a young baseball player just starting out, a fan of the game, or simply someone who enjoys reading about triumph and perseverance. Each page will transport you to a world where dreams come true-- where a single swing of the bat can alter history and the power of the human spirit shines brightly.

Within these thrilling pages, you will encounter the uplifting stories of 30 extraordinary individual players and their triumphant moments. These tales will transport you to the heart of the action, allowing you to experience the thrill of victory and the unyielding determination that drove these players to overcome impossible odds. Each story will serve as a testament to the tremendous spirit that exists in the world of baseball.

So, pick up your glove and cap, and prepare to embark on an exciting journey through the history of baseball with these extraordinary players. Allow their stories to inspire you, teach you valuable lessons, and ignite a deeper passion for the game.

Let's play ball!

Chapter 1

A No-Hitter Glory at Tiger Stadium – Nolan Ryan

S hadows covered the sacred grounds of Royals Stadium as the sun began to set over the city of Detroit. The stadium was electric with anticipation as the Angels and the Kansas City Royals played on May 15, 1973. Nobody could have predicted that one man, Nolan Ryan, would make this game legendary in baseball lore.

With the first pitch, the scene was set for an epic showdown. Right-handed fireballer Ryan ascended the mound, his gaze locked on the catcher's mitt in the background. His fame as a strikeout machine and mound master preceded him, but today he would cement his place in baseball lore.

Born Lynn Nolan Ryan Jr. on January 31, 1947, in Refugio, Texas, Nolan Ryan is an all-time great in baseball for his dominance on the mound and his incredible endurance as a player. Ryan was one of the best and longest-lasting pitchers in Major League Baseball history, with a career spanning an incredible 27 seasons.

When Ryan was a high school pitcher in Alvin, Texas, he showed glimpses of his future greatness. The New York Mets signed him in 1965 after being impressed by his blistering fastball, which regularly topped 100 miles per hour.

Nolan Ryan's early career was marred by struggles with commanding his pitches. After breaking into the big leagues in 1966, his high walk rates and occasional wildness raised concerns about his control of his powerful fastball. Others doubted his longevity and questioned whether or not his remarkable speed would hold up over time.

Nonetheless, Nolan Ryan was able to rise above his hardships and hone his skills to become one of baseball's all-time great pitchers. He put in countless hours with pitching coaches working to perfect his form and gain command of the ball. Ryan's dedication to training and preparation paid off when he was able to keep his sizzling fastball and add a lethal curveball and changeup to his arsenal.

Nolan Ryan was able to prove his doubters wrong as his career proceeded, becoming widely recognized as one of baseball's all-time great pitchers. Ryan showed flashes of tremendous talent in his first season with the Mets in 1968. His explosive combination of fastball and curveball confused hitters and made him a force to be reckoned with. Ryan's fastball would gain legendary status throughout the course of his career, inspiring dread in the hearts of even the best batters.

In 1972, Ryan was traded to the California Angels, where he truly began to carve out his place in baseball history. It was during his tenure with the Angels that he achieved some of his most remarkable accomplishments.

On May 15, 1973, Ryan threw his first of an astounding seven no-hitters, a record that still stands to this day. His reputation as a dominant force only grew as he consistently led the league in strikeouts, earning him the nickname "The Ryan Express."

With each pitch, the tension mounted. The Royals' hitters, formidable in their own right, stood no chance against Ryan's blistering fastball and a curveball that seemed to defy the laws of physics. The stadium hummed with a mixture of awe and unease as Ryan toyed with the opposing batters, striking them out one after another.

Ryan's dominance grew from inning to inning. His fiercely thrown fastball whizzed by the Royals' batters' bats, sending them swinging in vain. As the number of batters struck out kept rising, the crowd watched in awe. The air was thick with the anticipation of something truly spectacular happening.

The stadium went silent as the game neared the late innings. The crowd leaned forward, their gaze fixed on Ryan, who was on the verge of making history. Once cocky and belligerent, the Royals were now helpless bystanders as Ryan continued to dominate play.

The stakes were highest in the bottom of the ninth. The spectators stood to their feet, their voices rising in unison in a show of support and admiration. Ryan, calm and collected, was about to set out on his last mission to achieve immortality.

Feeling the pressure of the moment, Ryan looked down at the Royals' batters. The first hitter walked into the box with determination, knowing he didn't want to go down in obscurity. When Ryan launched an incomprehensible pitch, the batter swung frantically, but it was already too late. White as a ghost, the ball narrowly missed the bat.

One out.

The stadium shook with the thunder of the crowd's roaring applause. Ryan was unflappable as he geared up for the next battle.

Ryan kept up his assault on history with each pitch and each batter he faced. The crowd roared with appreciation after each strikeout, creating a beautiful harmony of praise. Once fearsome opponents, the Royals' batters now appeared to be little more than chess pieces in Ryan's pursuit of greatness.

The crowd waited nervously as the final two outs were recorded. The air was heavy with the significance of the situation. Ryan moved into his windup and then cracked his arm, releasing a pitch that was beyond anyone's ability to comprehend. The batter swung wildly but was unable to catch up to the speeding ball. He stood there in stunned silence as the ball sailed past his bat by a matter of inches.

Strike three!

The stadium quickly descended into chaos. The crowd went wild with excitement-- their cheers echoing through the starry night. Ryan's teammates raced to embrace him. Nolan Ryan had just thrown his first no-hitter, forever cementing his place in baseball lore!

Ryan took in the roaring acclaim of the crowd as he stood on the mound, a wave of exhilaration flooding over him. It was an astounding achievement that would be spoken about for years to come.

A spellbinding exhibition of dominance and determination, Nolan Ryan's no-hitter in 1973 was unforgettable. Baseball fans would talk about that day for years to come, praising the determination of one player and his dedication to excellence.

Chapter 2
A Triumph at Ebbets Field – Jackie Robinson

On April 15, 1947, in the crisp spring air, the grounds of Ebbets Field were buzzing with anticipation. As the Brooklyn Dodgers prepared to take on the Boston Braves and make history, the stands were filled with whispers of a cultural revolution. Jackie Robinson, who carried the weight of social change on his shoulders, was the center of attention.

Jackie Robinson was an American professional baseball player who became an iconic figure in breaking the color barrier in Major League Baseball. Born on January 31, 1919, in Cairo, Georgia. Robinson's legacy is about his resilience, tenacity, and commitment to social change, as well as his achievements on the field.

Robinson's professional baseball career began in 1945, when he joined the Kansas City Monarchs. Branch Rickey, the general manager of the Brooklyn Dodgers, was immediately drawn to his competitive abilities as an all-around athlete and talent for stealing bases.

Jackie Robinson's ability to turn hardship into motivation had a significant impact on his development as a batter in Major League Baseball. He was the first African-American player in the league, and as such, he was subjected to intense scrutiny and pressure to succeed. Instead of letting these obstacles slow him down, Robinson used them as fuel to become a better hitter. He was able to convert the stress into a ruthless desire to achieve thanks to his strong will and ability to concentrate. Each at-bat became a chance to prove his worth and combat the negative prejudices made about him because of his race.

On April 15, 1947, Robinson made history by becoming the first African-American player in Major League Baseball when he made his debut for the Brooklyn Dodgers. His arrival in the largely white league was faced with bigotry and hatred from fans, opponents, and even some teammates. Despite many death threats and verbal abuse, Robinson remained calm and concentrated on his game.

Robinson's development as a batter was fueled by his ability to gain insight from his mistakes. Instead of becoming disheartened by setbacks, he meticulously analyzed his at-bats, identifying areas for improvement and making the necessary adjustments. His legendary work ethic and commitment were evident in his relentless pursuit of excellence and practice. Despite confronting racism and prejudice, he used these obstacles as motivation to advance. He approached each game with an intense desire to disprove his critics.

Robinson's focus on team success, in addition to his individual goals, was crucial to his development as a batter. He understood the significance of contributing to his team's victories and used that understanding as motivation to become a more efficient hitter. Robinson maintained composure at the plate despite the obstacles he faced, making better judgments and maintaining a positive attitude.

In the end, Jackie Robinson's ability to use adversity as a catalyst for development and improvement enabled him to overcome racial barriers and become one of MLB's most influential and successful players. Beyond his on-field accomplishments, his legacy is a testament to the strength of determination, resilience, and perseverance in the face of adversity.

Throughout his career, Robinson continuously demonstrated his exceptional playing abilities. He was a six-time All-Star, earned the National League MVP Award in 1949, and instrumental in helping the Dodgers achieve six National League pennants and their first World Series title in 1955.

On April 15, 1947, Robinson stood at the threshold of fate as the sun began its descent and cast an amber light across the diamond. It was time for him to confront the prejudice and animosity that had plagued the sport for too long. He understood that this game would be more than a battle between bat and ball; it was battle on the grand stage of America's pastime.

At bat, Robinson's pulse pounded in his chest as he assumed his position, feeling the pressure of history. The pitcher cocked his arm and unleashed a fastball toward him. Robinson focused his attention with a steely gaze, his bat poised to administer his own brand of force.

The stadium suddenly echoed with the sound of wood striking leather as Robinson made solid contact with the ball. Like a bolt of lightning, Robinson dashed towards first base with his legs a blur of speed and determination as the ball ascended into the outfield. The roar of the crowd grew louder, causing a wave of emotion to wash over him. This was more than a success; it was a resounding assertion that talent was not bound by race.

Robinson faced not only opposing pitchers in each successive at-bat, but also the demons of prejudice that sought to break his spirit. After each pitch, he remained steadfast, his resolve unwavering. His supporters' applause mingled with the jeers of those clinging to a divided past. Robinson, however, remained focused, drawing strength from his conviction that his mere presence on the field was a beacon of optimism for a better future.

In the late innings, with the score tied, Robinson found himself on second base with a pounding pulse. The pitcher threw a vicious curveball that sliced through the air. Robinson, undeterred, anticipated the pitch, guided by his intuition. He erupted from first base at blinding speed, rounded the bases and slid into home plate with a jubilant roar. The umpire's hand then shot into the air, signaling a safe play.

The audience applauded in a tumultuous symphony, its thunderous clamor shaking the very foundations of Ebbets Field. Jackie Robinson had not only conquered the game, but he had also overcome racial discrimination. At that moment of glory, the baseball diamond became a battlefield where bravery and tenacity triumphed over hatred.

Robinson stood on the field as the last out was made and the Dodgers were declared winners against the Braves, his chest heaving with exertion and ecstasy. He had broken down barriers with just one game and written his name in stone. Jackie Robinson was now more than just a baseball player; he was a symbol of human solidarity and an inspiration to millions.

As the sun went down on that fateful April day, everyone understood that baseball had undergone a profound change. The game would never be the same again; a new hero had emerged, demonstrating that skill, bravery, and the boldness to dream could bring about revolutionary change.

Chapter 3
A Grand Slam Debut at Fenway – Daniel Nava

The scene was set on a warm summer night at Fenway Park. The game on June 12, 2010, would go down in baseball lore as the night Daniel Nava wrote his name in the record books. There was a heavy atmosphere of expectation as the Boston Red Sox took the field. Undrafted free agent Nava stood in the on-deck circle. He had worked hard to make it to the big leagues—and here he was, at the pinnacle of his years of effort and perseverance.

The game progressed with the usual rhythm of shattering bats and popping gloves. Bases loaded, Nava came up to bat in the second inning. He felt the pressure rising as he pressed his cleats into the batter's box. The opposing pitcher ramped up to throw a fastball with all his might.

Time slowed as Nava's focus narrowed on the ball and his senses sharpened.

He was ready to make history...

Nava always had a soft spot for the game of baseball. However, the road he took to the major leagues was hardly an easy one. Nava was a talented player, but he was passed over by scouts from Division I schools and never offered a scholarship. However, he was unfazed by this setback and enrolled in the College of San Mateo, where he continued to develop his baseball skills and show off his talents.

Nava attended Santa Clara University in 2003 with the hopes of playing baseball, but did not make the team. After Nava finished college, his dream for pursuing a career in professional baseball seemed bleak after failing to receive offers from the major league.

Nava's perseverance was tested, but he used these obstacles as stepping stones to become a stronger hitter. Nava keep his resolve as he advanced through the minor leagues. Given that he lacked the advantage of a distinguished draft status, proving himself in this competitive environment required unwavering dedication and perseverance. Nonetheless, Nava's work ethic and resolve remained unshaken. He devoted countless hours to honing his hitting skills and continuously sought methods to improve. As he advanced through the minor divisions, he demonstrated adaptability by learning from his experiences and modifying his batting approach.

Nonetheless, Nava's determination paid off when he impressed scouts from the Boston Red Sox during a trial in 2007. The Red Sox, seeing potential in his abilities and work ethic, signed him as an undrafted free agent, allowing him to fulfill his ambition of playing in the major leagues.

Nava's journey was greatly impacted by his mental fortitude. The unpredictability of his future could have easily discouraged him, but he maintained a positive attitude and remained focused on his ultimate objective of playing in the major divisions. When the opportunity eventually presented itself with the Boston Red Sox, he grabbed it with both hands and made an immediate impact in his debut, etching his name into the books of Major League Baseball history.

The night of June 12th, 2010 was the moment that Nava's hard work paid off. The Boston Red Sox rookie took the pitch from Phillies pitcher Joe Blanton and swung fluidly-- the sound of his bat cracking reverberated across the stadium. The ball soared through the warm night air.

As it flew beautifully over the right-field wall, the fans erupted in a roar of applause and shock.

It was a home run!

During this incredible moment, it seemed as if time had stopped. The walls of Fenway Park echoed with the fans' united joy as the stadium rocked with anticipation.

Completing the third base turn, Nava felt his heart pumping and spirits soar. The crowd's applause reverberated in his head, giving him strength to keep going. As he touched home plate, his teammates rushed to embrace him, their own excitement mirrored in his.

Daniel Nava did something incredible on his Major League debut. Nava's emotions surged, the climax of every hardship, every uncertainty, and every ounce of persistence that had taken him to this extraordinary achievement. His fellow players high-fived him ecstatically, witnessing an unbelievable feat. Daniel Nava was now entwined into the very fabric of baseball history.

Nava's grand slam at Fenway Park was more than just a baseball feat. It had become a metaphor for perseverance and faith in one's own abilities-- a symbol of the victory of the human spirit. Daniel Nava had become a role model for anybody who dared to dream big, proving that everything was possible with enough hard work and determination.

Chapter 4
The Iron Horse's Greatest Day – Lou Gehrig

O n June 3, 1932, the New York Yankees traveled to Philadelphia's famed Shibe Park to take on their longtime rivals, the Philadelphia Athletics. Baseball fans were buzzing with excitement as they took their seats in the stands, knowing they were about to witness a titanic showdown.

Lou Gehrig, a man who had come to represent strength and willpower, was among the Yankees' starting lineup. The tall first baseman walked up to the plate, his quiet confidence shadowing his imposing stature. The ballpark was about to witness a historic moment, but nobody knew it yet.

With a fire of determination, Gehrig stepping into the batter's box as the first pitch was delivered. There was a collective gasp from the crowd as all eyes focused on the sacred number 4.

Born in New York City on June 19, 1903, Lou Gehrig is widely regarded as one baseball's all-time greats. He has shown extraordinary athletic ability throughout his life, as well as remarkable perseverance.

Gehrig first began his legendary career while attending Columbia University, where he was an outstanding first baseman and a powerful hitter. In 1923, the New York Yankees saw potential in him and signed him to a professional contract. From the moment he stepped foot on the Yankee Stadium field, Lou Gehrig was destined to become a baseball legend. Famous for his tremendous strength, Gehrig rose rapidly to prominence as a prolific home run hitter, regularly knocking in runs, and providing a solid force to the Yankees lineup.

Due to his endless stamina and work ethic, Lou Gehrig was known as "The Iron Horse." He broke records by appearing in 2,130 consecutive games during his career. Everyone from his teammates to his opponents to the fans respected and admired him for his consistently high level of play.

Through a combination of natural talent and unwavering commitment, Gehrig constantly sought to improve his batting skills. Gehrig never rested on his laurels, despite the fact that his exceptional talents provided a solid foundation for his development as a hitter. His approach was characterized by diligent practice, as he spent countless hours perfecting his swing and technique.

As a keen observer of the game, Gehrig studied other pitchers' patterns to gain a competitive edge, learning from veteran players and coaches. Equally important was his mental approach; Gehrig remained patient at the plate, waiting for the ideal pitches to drive while maintaining composure under stress. As pitchers adapted their strategies to counter him, Gehrig adapted his striking approach accordingly, demonstrating his flexibility. Physical fitness played a crucial role in Gehrig's hitting prowess, providing him with the strength and stamina to excel over lengthy and demanding seasons. His optimistic outlook and unwavering determination further distinguished him, establishing him as a genuine baseball legend.

In 1927, Gehrig become a member of the Yankees' "Murderers' Row". With the help of other great Yankees hitters like Babe Ruth, the Yankees won their first World Series.

Tragically, Gehrig's brilliant career was cut short. The diagnosis of amyotrophic lateral sclerosis (ALS), a degenerative and irreversible neurological condition, in 1939 put an end to Gehrig's playing career.

Before sorrow could set in, however, Gehrig made history at Shibe Park on June 3, 1932.

The stakes were raised with each pitch and hit as the game progressed. With his eyes fixed on the pitcher and a bead of sweat running down his temple, Gehrig stepped up to the bat. The first pitch came flying his way, and in one seamless action, Gehrig let go with his bat, making solid contact with the ball with a loud crack. The spectators held their breath as the ball sailed over the outfield wall and into the stands for a home run.

Despite the awe-inspiring nature of his first home run, Gehrig was just warming up. With each new bat at plate, the crowd's energy level increased dramatically. Pitchers for the Athletics feared Gehrig's power and struggled to match it. Three more spectacular home runs later, Gehrig swung with all his might and sent the ball screaming out of the park. As if the ball itself had surrendered to Gehrig's dominance, his fourth home run left a trail of awe in its aftermath.

Fans from both teams, united by their passion for the sport, stood to acclaim Gehrig's extraordinary display of strength. The tension that had been building throughout the game had reached its climax, and Gehrig stood in the center of it all, basking in the adulation of the crowd. No other American League player had ever hit four home runs in a single contest before him.

The Yankees prevailed with a resounding 20-13 victory, but Gehrig's performance will be remembered in the books of baseball history. That historic day in Shibe Park, Lou Gehrig's brilliance showed brightly, reminding everyone why he was known as "The Iron Horse."

At the sound of the final out being recorded, Gehrig walked off the field, a hero in the eyes of the crowd who had just witnessed his unprecedented achievement. The impact of his victory resonated through the ages, engraving his reputation in the minds of baseball fans and establishing him as one of the sport's most revered and famous players.

Chapter 5
The Laser-like Arm – Roberto Clemente

Game 7 of the 1971 World Series was a nail-biter, with both the Pittsburgh Pirates and the Baltimore Orioles showcasing remarkable talent and skill. The strain in the air was apparent as the decisive game neared. The Pirates aimed to win the championship, driven by Roberto Clemente's unshakable determination.

With the game deadlocked in the fourth inning, Clemente strolled into the batter's box, his focus steady. As he faced Orioles pitcher Mike Cuellar, history was about to be made...

Roberto Clemente Walker was born in Carolina, Puerto Rico, on August 18, 1934. He grew up in a low-income family and developed his love of baseball at a young age—so much, in fact that Clemente's talent rapidly drew the notice of scouts signing him with the Brooklyn Dodgers at the age of 20, however he was sent to the minor leagues that same year.

The next year, however, Clemente's major league debut occurred on April 17, 1955 with the Pittsburgh Pirates. He soon established himself as one of the league's top outfielders, demonstrating strong abilities both at the plate and in the field. Clemente's throwing arm was famous, and his precision became a trademark of his game.

Early in his career, Roberto Clemente encountered several obstacles that tested his determination and dedication to the sport he cherished. Having grown up in Puerto Rico and speaking Spanish as his first language, the language barrier was one of the greatest obstacles he faced. During his early years in the minor leagues, it was difficult for him to communicate with his colleagues and coaches because of this. Additionally, Clemente faced ethnic discrimination and prejudice, which were regrettably prevalent in baseball during his era. However, instead of giving in to these obstacles, Clemente used them to motivate his determination to succeed.

Roberto Clemente's exceptional arm and throwing ability distinguished him as one of the game's finest outfielders and became a defining aspect of his playing style. Clemente relied on natural aptitude, extensive practice, and a strong work ethic to develop his remarkable throw. As a child, he participated in numerous sports, including track and field and basketball, which contributed to his overall athleticism.

However, it was his commitment to practicing his throwing technique that allowed him to truly refine his skills. Clemente devoted innumerable hours to improving his arm strength and accuracy, as well as his throwing mechanics.

His dedication to perfecting his throw, both in training and in games, enabled him to develop a cannon arm that was dreaded by baserunners and respected by opponents. Clemente received many honors and achievements throughout his career—he was nominated to the All-Star team 15 times and won 12 Gold Glove Awards for his skilled play in right field. He also won the National League Most Valuable Player Award in 1966, establishing himself as one of the game's best players at the time.

On that fateful day in Game 7, while facing Orioles pitcher Mike Cuellar, Clemente connected with a pitch and sent it soaring over the outfield wall for a home run. The crowd erupted into a frenzy of cheers and applause, witnessing Clemente's clutch performance in a pivotal moment of the game.

But Clemente's heroics were not limited to his offensive prowess. As the game unfolded, his extraordinary defensive skills came to the forefront. In the bottom of the fourth inning, with the Orioles threatening to take the lead, Clemente made an incredible throw from right field, gunning down a runner at home plate. It was a pivotal play that changed the course of the game and swung the momentum in favor of the Pirates.

With each passing inning, Clemente's influence grew stronger. He continued to make key defensive plays, robbing the Orioles of potential hits and turning them into outs. His arm, known for its laser-like accuracy, intimidated baserunners, forcing them to think twice before taking an extra base.

Clemente's impact extended beyond his on-field heroics. His presence alone in the lineup provided a spark of inspiration to his teammates, pushing them to give their all and leave nothing on the field. His leadership and unwavering determination were catalysts for the Pirates' eventual win.

In the end, the Pirates claimed the World Series championship with a score of 2-1. This iconic game displayed Clemente's exceptional talent and ability to deliver in tense moments. It showcased his all-around skills as both an offensive force and a defensive player, solidifying his place among the greatest players in baseball history.

Chapter 6
A Home Run First at Busch Stadium – Hank Aaron

There was an air of excitement at Busch Stadium on April 23, 1954. It was set to be an exciting game between the Milwaukee Braves and the St. Louis Cardinals, two teams that had long been bitter rivals. Nobody could have predicted that this day would come to represent one man's greatness-- a player named Hank Aaron.

"Hammerin' Hank" Aaron is widely considered to be one of the best baseball players of all time. His baseball career began in 1951 with the Indianapolis Clowns, where he played for three months. He then joined the Boston Braves in 1952 when he was just 18 years old.

After making his Major League Baseball debut in 1954, Aaron was immediately recognized as a formidable opponent. His compact, powerful swing earned him the nickname "Hammerin' Hank". His superior hand-eye coordination allowed him to consistently make strong contact and drive the ball with pinpoint accuracy.

Hank Aaron's early career was marked by numerous setbacks that put his tenacity and resilience to the test. He experienced the harsh realities of racial segregation and discrimination as an African-American player trying to break into major league baseball in the 1950s. Aaron's early development may have been hindered by his lack of exposure to top-tier competition while he was in the segregated leagues. In addition, as a black player in a predominately white league, the weight of the expectations placed upon Aaron after Jackie Robinson's breakthrough was significant.

Despite these setbacks, Hank Aaron's remarkable batting skills were shaped by his dedication and work ethic. Although he had a natural hitting ability, he never let his guard down. Instead, Aaron spent many hours honing his swing in an effort to enhance its timing and mechanics. He had a methodical and deliberate approach at the plate, studying the habits of opposing pitchers in order to exploit their weaknesses. Because of his remarkable mental fortitude, Aaron was able to stay cool under intense pressure and hit with both power and consistency. He was also eager to improve as a batter, as evidenced by his openness to instruction and suggestions from more seasoned players.

When Hank Aaron was a rookie with the Milwaukee Braves in 1954, he had a breakout season that included some of the best games of his career. On April 23, Aaron forever changed baseball when he faced the St. Louis Cardinals at Busch Stadium.

People settled into their seats as the game began, all of them staring intently at Aaron's calm, collected demeanor. The stakes were rising with each pitch, and the air was thick with the intensity of the event. Aaron, the embodiment of concentration, took the first pitch from Cardinals ace Vic Raschi and swung powerfully.

A resounding "crack" could be heard all throughout the stadium as the ball sailed high into the clear blue sky. A beautiful home run to spark the Braves' offense! It quickly brought the crowd to its feet in a shared expression of awe. The scene was set as Aaron gave a riveting performance.

The crowd was soon captivated by his every action, and the suspense grew with each inning. As the sixth inning began, the Cardinals were terrified of Aaron's reign. As Aaron stepped up to the plate, the stadium waited, their hearts collectively beating.

When Raschi threw his pitch, Aaron made contact with a loud snap that defied physics. The ball blasted off his bat and was sent on its way up to the sky. Everyone in the stadium held their breath as Aaron hit his third home run, completing a historic trifecta.

Chaos broke out in the stadium. The crowd erupted into loud cheers that echoed throughout the arena. At just 20 years old, Hank Aaron wrote himself into the history books with his first major league home run.

Throughout the rest of the game, Aaron's brilliance shone brightly, impressing everyone in attendance. The Braves defeated the Cardinals by a score of 7-5, and the team will always be remembered for Aaron's legendary effort. On that fateful day in April, Hank Aaron displayed a level of baseball greatness that defied explanation by natural means. The game in which he hit three home runs was a watershed moment in his legendary career, cementing his place as one of baseball's all-time greats.

Chapter 7
An Impossible Record Broken -
Cal Ripken Jr

Camden Yards was illuminated by the late summer sun on September 6, 1995. There was a sense of magic in the air, for on this night Cal Ripken Jr. stood on the brink of immortality. He was one game away from breaking Lou Gehrig's legendary consecutive games played streak.

The atmosphere was solemn as the fans filed into the stadium. Ripken, affectionately known as "The Iron Man," won the hearts of spectators all over the world with his tireless dedication to baseball and his legendary toughness. The entire stadium seemed to be staring at him in anticipation of this historic moment.

Early in his career, Cal Ripken Jr. encountered obstacles that tested his drive and determination. The burden of living up to the legacy of his father, Cal Ripken Sr., a respected baseball coach and manager for the Baltimore Orioles, was one of the most significant obstacles he faced. The pressure to follow in his father's footsteps could have been overpowering for Ripken Jr., but he was intent on forging his own path. In addition, he labored with injuries during his early years in the minor leagues, which impeded his development and raised questions about his ability to remain healthy and reach his full potential.

The development of Cal Ripken Jr.'s skills as a batter was the result of his unwavering dedication to hard work and continuous advancement. He had a strong work ethic, devoting numerous hours of practice and repetition to developing his hitting skills. Ripken Jr. adopted a disciplined approach at the plate, focusing on pitch selection and culti-vating an acute eye for strikes. His remarkable hitting consistency was a result of his ability to make adjustments and adapt to different pitching approaches. In addition, Ripken Jr. sought advice from veteran instructors and team-mates, demonstrating his eagerness to improve as a batter. As a result of his commitment and perseverance, Cal Ripken Jr. became one of the most accomplished and admired hitters in baseball history, leaving a lasting legacy as one of the sport's genuine legends.

Cal Ripken Jr. set a major league baseball record by appearing in 2,632 consecutive games. His tenure with the Baltimore Orioles was emblematic of his reliability, longevity, and commitment to baseball. Ripken's dedication to turning up and giving his all every day is an example of a strong work ethic for athletes and non-athletes alike.

Cal Ripken Jr.'s streak began in 1982, where the air at Exhibition Stadium in Toronto was dense with anticipation. The Baltimore Orioles were in town to play the Toronto Blue Jays, and no one knew that this seemingly ordinary game would be the start of an extraordinary journey. That day, the Orioles roster included the youthful and determined shortstop. Since joining the team, he had demonstrated promise and potential, but today fate had something extraordinary in store for him. As Mark Belanger, the Orioles' regular starting shortstop, nursed an injury, the manager made a fateful decision by giving Ripken the chance to flourish.

As soon as Ripken strode onto the field that day, he was overcome with determination. He understood that this opportunity could be the turning point in his career, and he was determined to seize it. He assumed his position at shortstop with a steady hand and a focused mind, prepared for whatever challenges lie ahead.

As the game progressed, Ripken demonstrated his extraordinary talent and composure. He appeared to be in perfect sync with the game's tempo, gliding across the field and making plays that astounded the spectators. As the final inning approached, Ripken remained on the field, his pulse pounding with excitement and apprehension.

On that day, the Orioles did not win, but little did anyone realize that something much more significant had occurred.

This game set Cal Ripken Jr. on a path that would permanently alter his life and baseball history. Unprecedented in its nature, he had begun a streak of consecutive games.

Days became weeks, weeks became months, and months became years, but Cal Ripken Jr. continued to play in every Orioles game. His winning run became a symbol of his commitment, tenacity, and unwavering dedication to the sport he cherished. He played despite minor aches and injuries, exceeding his limits day after day and season after season.

As the years progressed, Ripken's streak garnered momentum and captivated fans and the media. The entire world was in awe as he broke Lou Gehrig's record of 2,130 consecutive games on September 6, 1995. Ripken etched his name deeper into the record books and the affections of baseball fans worldwide with each game he played.

Ripken's winning sequence remained intact in the face of adversity. On his determined course, injuries that would have sidelined others were mere obstacles. His enthusiasm for the game and unwavering loyalty to his comrades propelled him to overcome every obstacle that arose.

The nickname "Iron Man" was given to him in recognition of his extraordinary accomplishments and unyielding character. He became a symbol of inspiration by demonstrating that anything was possible with talent, perseverance, and an undying passion for the game.

Thus, on that fateful day in 1982 in Toronto, a legend was created. Cal Ripken Jr.'s streak of consecutive games played began, and it would continue for more than 16 seasons and 2,632 games-- a testament to his unwavering commitment to baseball and his status as one of the sport's finest players. As the world marveled at his accomplishments, one thing became abundantly clear-- Cal Ripken Jr.'s legacy was indelibly engraved in the hearts and minds of baseball fans, a tribute to the power of perseverance and the enchantment of the game itself.

Chapter 8
The Called Shot & Ruth's Day at Sportsman's Park – Babe Ruth

The scene was set at Chicago's Wrigley Field in the fall of 1932, where a rowdy crowd filled the stadium. The Yankees were determined to even the series after the Cubs won the first two games. Immense pressure was laid on Babe Ruth's broad shoulders as he stepped into the batter's box.

The stage was set in the first inning-- two outs and a runner on second. Ruth fearlessly faced the intensity of Cubs pitcher Charlie Root. In a bold move, he raised his right arm and gestured toward the center field bleachers as if to announce his intentions. The crowd began to stir as they realized something truly remarkable was about to occur.

"Babe Ruth," or George Herman Ruth Jr., was born on February 6, 1895, and is widely regarded as baseball's best player. His powerful hitting earned him the nicknames

"Sultan of Swat" and "The Great Bambino"-- both of which he deservedly earned. His legacy developed as he set numerous records while playing for the Boston Red Sox and the New York Yankees. Ruth's charisma, towering stature, and record-breaking home runs changed baseball forever.

Due to his unconventional playing style and rebellious temperament, Babe Ruth endured criticism throughout his career, particularly in the beginning. Ruth's unconventional approach to hitting and pitching stood in stark contrast to the traditional manner of the era when he first appeared on the scene as a young player. Critics questioned his swing mechanics and doubted that his powerful yet apparently undisciplined approach could be successful over the long haul.

The media and baseball fans routinely criticized Ruth's off-field conduct. Some questioned his commitment to the sport and whether he could maintain a successful career despite his lifestyle, as his reputation for partying contrasted with the more conservative values of the time. In addition, as Ruth transitioned from pitcher to full-time hitter, some questioned his ability to excel as a position player. Concerns were raised about his defensive abilities, and skeptics questioned whether he could maintain his hitting prowess consistently.

However, Babe Ruth disproved his critics with his outstanding performances on the field. He revolutionized baseball with his extraordinary power-hitting abilities and became a beloved figure, winning over supporters and ultimately silencing naysayers with his historic accomplishments.

One of Babe Ruth's most iconic games took place on October 1, 1932, during Game 3 of the World Series between the New York Yankees and the Chicago Cubs-- A game that would forever cement Ruth's legend and add another chapter to his remarkable career.

As Charlie Root made his pitch, the pressure was at an all-time high. Ruth swung ferociously and connected with great force. The ball rose into the sky, carrying the aspirations of a whole city. The outfield wall was easily cleared, and the ball ended up deep in the spectator stands, scoring a home run.

The fifth inning was when Ruth really started to shine. Ruth came back up to bat after they had tied the game. Everyone in the crowd stood up, their pulses racing. Knowing the stakes, Charlie Root attempted to outsmart the heavy hitter. Ruth had the count at two strikes before he smashed the next pitch out of the ballpark and into the night sky.

The ball went soaring through the air like an unstoppable meteor. Awe spread throughout the stadium as it flew over the outfield wall. In World Series history, no player had ever hit two home runs in a single game. The applause and cheers from the crowd echoed loudly in the night.

Ruth hit two home runs during his historic performance, helping the Yankees win a pivotal third game of the series.

His immense strength, imposing persona, and ability to rise to the challenge in crucial moments were on full display. That day, Babe Ruth's legacy was further cemented, and his name permanently etched into baseball history.

Debate still persists over whether or not Ruth actually called his shot before hitting the immortal home run. Nevertheless, the game further established Ruth as a sports legend.

Babe Ruth had another famous game on October 6, 1926-- Game 4 of the World Series when the New York Yankees and the St. Louis Cardinals fought for the title. This date would be known as "The Babe Ruth Game" in history due to Ruth's performance under intense pressure.

The atmosphere was electric with excitement. The Cardinals had a two-game lead in the series, and the situation was dire. The Yankees were down and out and were hoping their charismatic slugger, Babe Ruth, could pull off a miracle. The atmosphere at Sportsman's Park was tense as the game progressed. The Cardinals and Yankees fought fiercely, with the fate of the World Series riding on the seams of every pitch. But the stage was set for Ruth's heroics in the top of the ninth inning.

The crowd went wild as Ruth stepped into the batter's box with the score tied at two runs each and his stance wide and commanding. Grover Cleveland Alexander, the Cardinals' ace, looked at him with a mixture of admiration and intent.

It was about to be showtime in the epic face off between these two legendary figures.

The pressure was building with each pitch. Alexander threw everything he had at Ruth, including a variety of curveballs and fastballs. The crowd waited, their hearts collectively beating.

Then something happened.

Ruth swung with all the determination of a man who knew was destined for greatness. The sound of the bat breaking was a climax that reverberated through the stadium and into the ages.

After leaving the bat, the ball shot skyward. As it gracefully traced an arc through the dwindling light, the world appeared to stop turning. The ball went over the fence and into left field—proof of Ruth's supernatural power. An enormous roar rose from the crowd as applause mingled with astonishment.

The stadium was alive with excitement as Ruth rounded third with a broad grin on his face. The city's hopes and dreams, along with the weight of the game and the series, seemed to vanish into thin air. Ruth had pulled off the seemingly impossible, turning the tide in favor of the Yankees.

The game ended with the Yankees winning 10-5, but that score pales in comparison to the significance of Ruth's heroic feat. The aftershock of that play is still being felt today, and his name will forever be remembered as one of baseball's all-time greats. It was a dramatic scene that captured Ruth's ability to take center stage and change the outcome of a game with a single powerful swing.

That day in October would go down in history as the day Babe Ruth further cemented his place in baseball lore. It was a showcase of everything that made him great: his talent, his charisma, and his ability to perform brilliantly under pressure.

Chapter 9
A New Rookie Record – Ichiro Suzuki

On April 2, 2001, the excitement in Safeco Field was apparent as people waited for the game to begin. The Seattle Mariners, backed by their mysterious rookie sensation Ichiro Suzuki, were ready to take on the Oakland Athletics in the Opening Series. The air was charged with the anticipation of Japanese baseball fans who would finally get to see Ichiro perform on the grand stage of American Major League Baseball.

The spectators became quiet as the first pitch was about to be thrown, their gazes fixed on Ichiro.

He took a commanding stance at home plate, aware of the pressure that was on his shoulders. The pitcher unleashed a blazing fastball, and in a masterful display of timing and accuracy, Ichiro swung his bat.

Ichiro Suzuki, known simply as Ichiro, is a Japanese baseball player who made a significant impact in American major league baseball. He became the first player in MLB history to achieve 10 consecutive 200-hit seasons and is revered for his dedication, work ethic, and passion for the game.

Ichiro started his career in Japan, where he played for the Orix BlueWave. During that time, he established himself as one of the league's top players, earning many awards including seven consecutive batting titles and three MVP awards.

In 2001, Ichiro made the transition to American MLB, signing with the Seattle Mariners. It didn't take long for him to make an impact-- in his first season, he earned both the American League Rookie of the Year and the AL MVP awards, becoming the first player to achieve simultaneous wins.

Early in his career, Ichiro Suzuki encountered unusual obstacles, mostly due to cultural and linguistic differences. He was one of the first Japanese position players to succeed in MLB after making the difficult shift from Japan. Because of his unfamiliarity with American baseball and language, he found the transition to be challenging. His potential to succeed at the MLB level was also questioned by those who were skeptical that his hitting approach, which prioritized contact and speed over power, would be successful in the majors.

Ichiro, however, overcame these challenges and developed his outstanding batting talents due to his extraordinary work ethic and tenacity. He was born with a slap-hitting style and an ability to hit the ball all over the field. However, Ichiro's on-field achievements were also due to his continued pursuit of improvement. He kept up an intense training schedule, spending countless hours honing his swing and technique. Discipline at the plate gave him mastery of the bat and made him a formidable opponent for pitchers. Ichiro's dedication to mastering American baseball and his willingness to listen to instruction from his coaches and teammates were other crucial factors in his growth.

Ichiro Suzuki was able to become one of baseball's all-time best hitters and a cultural hero in Japan and the United States thanks to his relentless determination and willingness to adapt.

Throughout his MLB career, Ichiro demonstrated an exceptional hitting ability. He became known for his unique batting stance and his ability to knock hits to all parts of the field. Ichiro's combination of power, precision, and speed made him a nightmare for opposing pitchers and a delight for fans to watch.

On April 6, 2001, the Seattle Mariners took to the field at the Texas Rangers' home, the Ballpark in Arlington, as the sun sank below the horizon.

Ichiro was about to confront a new challenge-- pitting himself against the best in the American baseball.

Ichiro was undeniably present on the field as the game progressed. He patrolled right field with grace and agility, exuding a high level of composure and concentration. With each inning, anticipation mounted, as everyone knew this young baseball prodigy was capable of something extraordinary.

And finally, the time came…

Ichiro approached the plate in the top of the third inning with his gaze fixed on Rangers pitcher Jeff Zimmerman. The audience became subdued, focusing their attention solely on the figure standing at the plate. Ichiro responded with a fluid and powerful stroke after Zimmerman threw a fastball in his direction.

The bat's crack reverberated throughout the stadium as the projectile flew high and far into right field. It was immediately clear that this was no ordinary strike; it was a home run! As Ichiro rounded the bases, the audience erupted in cheers and applause.

During that thrilling moment, Ichiro Suzuki inscribed his name into the record books of history. His first home run in the major leagues was more than a demonstration of physical power; it was a manifestation of his talent, determination, and pure enjoyment of the game. With this accomplishment, he announced to the baseball world that he had arrived and was prepared to take it by storm.

The remainder of Ichiro's inaugural year was nothing short of extraordinary. He exhibited an extraordinary ability, amassing hits at an unprecedented rate. His defensive abilities in right field were mesmerizing, as he displayed a rocket arm and extraordinary agility.

Ichiro's impact on the Mariners and the sport of baseball became undeniable as the season progressed. He was named American League Rookie of the Year and Most Valuable Player in the same season. Ichiro's achievements transcended cultural barriers, enthralling supporters not only in Seattle and Japan, but all over the world.

Chapter 10
A Tie Breaking Pitch – Sandy Koufax

In the early evening of October 14, 1965, the sun began to set over Dodger Stadium. Game 7 of the World Series between the Los Angeles Dodgers and the Minnesota Twins was played amidst rising tension. This moment was the climax of a long and difficult series of battles. But on that fateful night, Sandy Koufax was the center of attention.

Koufax's towering stature gave off an air of authority as he stepped onto the pitching mound. All season long, batters had been terrified by his blazing fastball and knee-buckling curveball. Everyone in the crowd held their breath in anticipation of what they knew was about to happen.

Born on December 30, 1935, Sandy Koufax was a dominant pitcher who played for both the Brooklyn and Los Angeles Dodgers from 1955 to 1966. Known for his blazing fastball and devastating curveball, Koufax had a remarkable career--winning three Cy Young Awards and leading the Dodgers to multiple World Series victories. He is considered one of the most dominant pitchers of all time and is revered for his remarkable skills and integrity both on and off the field.

Sandy Koufax encountered obstacles early in his career due to his lack of control and struggles with consistency as a pitcher. He flashed talent, but his unpredictability on the mound and problems controlling his powerful fastball restricted his success. Koufax's first few years in the Major Leagues were filled with dissatisfaction and uncertainty, with his performance frequently falling short of expectations. In addition, he was plagued by injuries, especially persistent arm difficulties, which cast doubt on his durability and long-term prospects as a pitcher.

Koufax's tenacity and work ethic, on the other hand, were critical in reviving his career. He sought advice from pitching instructor Johnny Podres, who assisted him in refining his mechanics and developing improved pitch control. Koufax worked extensively on his delivery, perfecting a more consistent and repeatable motion. He also added a nasty curveball to his arsenal, combining it with his explosive fastball to make a fearsome one-two punch. Because of his dedication to increasing his conditioning and arm strength, Koufax was able to overcome his injury problems and become a reliable and dominant pitcher.

Sandy Koufax changed himself from a struggling teenage pitcher to one of baseball's most dominant and renowned pitchers via devotion and perseverance. His incredible story demonstrates the power of hard effort and persistence in overcoming obstacles and attaining one's full potential. Koufax's influence on the game and legacy as one of the greatest pitchers of all time continue to inspire both young players and fans.

One of Sandy Koufax's most iconic games occurred on October 14, 1965, during Game 7 of the World Series-- a matchup between the Los Angeles Dodgers and the Minnesota Twins. It was a game that would become a defining moment in Koufax's career, solidifying his legacy as one of the most dominant pitchers in baseball.

Koufax was in command from the very first pitch. As soon as he released it, the ball began to move with uncanny accuracy. Usually fierce and confident at the plate, the Twins' hitters floundered in the face of Koufax's deliveries. The tension in the stadium increased as the batters continued to strike out.

Koufax's brilliance continued to grow from inning to inning. Every time he threw a powerful fastball or unhittable breaking ball, the crowd went wild in awe of his virtuosity. Koufax's capable left arm felt like it held the fate of the world with every pitch.

The score remained tied in a tense and nerve-wracking deadlock as the game progressed. The crowd was captivated by every pitch and swing, their hearts beating in time with the frenetic energy. The tension built with every out, and the atmosphere was electric.

However, the game's defining moment occurred in the top of the ninth inning where Koufax mustered all of his determination and talent to break the tie. There was a palpable buzz in the stadium that went far beyond the realm of the game itself.

Fast and erratic, Koufax's pitches had a distinctive crack. With everything riding on them, the Twins' hitters went down one by one, strikeout after strikeout. The crowd went wild with excitement as the crack of the catcher's mitt mingled with their cheers.

Inspired by Koufax's otherworldly outs, the Dodgers maintained their momentum all the way into the bottom of the ninth. They battled back and eventually prevailed, 2-0, eventually sealing the deal on a World Series title. Sandy Koufax was the night's hero, and the crowd's roar echoed through the darkness like a chorus of praise.

The magnitude of his Game 7 performance had gone far beyond the realm of sports-- it had evolved into a display of domination, a resounding tribute to the value of persistence and the success of the human will. Those lucky enough to witness Koufax's performance will always remember it as a legendary moment in baseball history.

Chapter 11
The Dive That Made History – Derek Jeter

On July 1, 2004, two of baseball's greatest teams, the New York Yankees and the Boston Red Sox, met in a game at Yankee Stadium played in the humid heat of the summer. There was an electric buzz in the air as everyone waited for the next bout between these two formidable opponents. The crowd was electric; they knew they were in for a showdown to remember.

Once the game started, everyone in the stadium could feel the tension rising. In the first few innings, the two teams battled it out to establish themselves as the better team. With the Yankees inching closer to taking the lead in the top of the third, the stage was set for a decisive moment that would go down in baseball history.

A Red Sox batter smashed a line drive into the left-center field gap, and the sound of the bat reverberated through the stadium. A crucial hit was imminent as the ball soared through the air. The crowd waited anxiously as the fate of the Yankees' season hung in the balance.

However, out of nowhere, Derek Jeter appeared. He kept his gaze fixed on the ball as he ran at the opening at a rate that defied all reason. At the peak of his dive, with his body fully extended as time stood still...

Derek Jeter, a professional baseball player born on June 26, 1974, played his entire career with the New York Yankees. Affectionately known as "The Captain," Jeter was the driving force behind the Yankees' success. He was named to the All-Star team numerous times and won five World Series. Professionalism, grace under pressure, and clutch hitting made Jeter one of the most beloved and respected athletes of his era.

Jeter's early success on the baseball field was indicative of his innate skills. At Kalamazoo Central High School in Michigan, he was a standout student and quickly caught the eye of college and professional scouts. The Yankees picked him with the sixth overall pick in the 1992 Major League Baseball Draft, beginning his rise to baseball greatness.

After making his MLB debut on May 29, 1995, Jeter quickly became an indispensable member of the Yankees' lineup. He was the model of a team captain and an inspiration to young athletes thanks to his superb fielding, extraordinary instincts, and clutch hitting.

While playing defense for the Yankees in his first full season in the Major Leagues, Jeter made a number of mistakes and was criticized for his lack of range and defensive prowess. There were others who didn't think he could hold his own as a starting shortstop in the majors.

Derek Jeter's integrity and work ethic, however, remained unshaken, and he used his failures as springboards for growth. He put in many hours of practice perfecting his footwork and fielding skills. With the help of coaches and more seasoned teammates, Jeter fine-tuned his defensive techniques, resulting in better positioning and more calculated play. Furthermore, he sought counsel from the game's all-time great shortstop, Ozzie Smith, who enlightened him on the nuances of playing at the highest level.

By focusing on his defense, Jeter was able to rapidly ascend to the level of an elite shortstop. He led by example and consistently delivered in the most important moments of games throughout his career with amazing defensive efforts. It says a lot about Jeter that he was able to overcome adversity early in his career and develop into a Gold Glove shortstop. One of the best shortstops of all time, he won five World Series titles and was named to the All-Star team 14 times.

His "Captain Clutch" moniker was earned thanks to his stellar play in crucial moments.

One of Derek Jeter's most iconic games took place on July 1, 2004, at Yankee Stadium in New York City between the Yankees and the rival Boston Red Sox--forever remembered as "The Dive."

In a breathtaking instant, Jeter defied gravity-- his outstretched glove made contact with the ball, the leather smacking into the pocket with a satisfying thud, all the while crashing into the stands. The crowd erupted in astonishment, their cheers an explosion of disbelief and admiration.

Jeter held on tightly, not wanting to let go of the ball. Every fan in the stadium knew they had just seen a play that would go down as one of baseball's all-time greats, and they stood in amazement.

Jeter's dive had a seismic effect. It injected a surge of energy into his teammates and sent a jolt of fear into the Red Sox. The Yankees had turned the tables and were now in a position of strength. From then on, Jeter's presence could be felt in every facet of the competition.

At-bat, Jeter's concentration grew stronger. His bat crackled with intent, and his defense was solid as a rock. The audience's pulses raced in tandem as they watched every dramatic pitch. It was now a contest of wills, and Jeter was leading the charge.

The Yankees eventually came out on top. Inspiring his teammates to emulate his tireless pursuit of greatness, Jeter's amazing defensive exploits set the stage. After the last out was made, the crowd exploded in cheers, filling the stadium with the sound of victory.

Jeter walked off the field with a modest smile on his face, demonstrating composure and leadership. With just one dive, he had shown his dedication to perfection and swung the momentum of the game in his favor. Baseball history would always remember "The Dive" as a moment when Derek Jeter rose to the challenge and cemented his place in the record books.

Chapter 12
A No-Hitter at Dodger Stadium – Clayton Kershaw

On June 18, 2014, as the Pacific sun set below the horizon, a golden light bathed Dodger Stadium. The atmosphere was electric as the Los Angeles Dodgers and Colorado Rockies were ready to play. Little did they know, they were about to see a historic performance-- a pitching feat that would forever be etched into the record books of baseball.

Born on March 19, 1988, Clayton Kershaw is a left-handed pitcher of exceptional skill who has spent his whole career with the Los Angeles Dodgers. Kershaw is one of baseball's most dominant pitchers and a multiple Cy Young Award winner thanks to his focused control, deadly breaking pitches, and commanding performances. Both on and off the field, he is looked up to as an example of professionalism due to his focus, drive, and generosity.

Clayton Kershaw encountered adversity early in his career, which shaped his path to becoming one of the most dominant pitchers in baseball. His struggles with command and control were one of the primary obstacles he faced. Throughout his first few seasons in the Major Leagues, Clayton Kershaw struggled with inconsistency, frequently dealing with high pitch counts and more walks than desired. Critics questioned whether he could reach his full potential as an exceptional pitcher in light of these early obstacles.

Clayton Kershaw's perseverance and work ethic were instrumental in overcoming these obstacles and improving his pitching abilities. He devoted himself to researching the art of pitching, consulting with veteran pitchers, and collaborating closely with the Dodgers' coaching staff. Kershaw made substantial adjustments to his mechanics, enabling him to better control his exceptional fastball and devastating breaking pitches. In addition, he developed a more disciplined approach to pitch selection, learning to exploit hitters' vulnerabilities and gaining a better handle on his pitch count.

In addition, Kershaw acknowledged the importance of analytics and technology in his performance analysis. Using data and video analysis, he identified enhancement opportunities and made the necessary adjustments. Kershaw has become one of the game's most dominant pitchers as a result of his data-driven approach, his uncommon talent, and his tireless dedication.

On June 18, 2014, Clayton Kershaw, the Dodgers' stoic ace with a lightning fast fastball, took the mound against the Colorado Rockies. The crowd was buzzing with anticipation. The Rockies, knowing they would be facing an opponent known for their offensive strength, prepared for battle.

Kershaw had an air of authority right from the opening pitch. His fastball blazed with intent, and his curveballs defied logic. Everyone in the audience leaned forward, transfixed by the fascinating ballet.

There was a stillness across the stadium as the innings progressed. Kershaw's skill turned into a show of astounding brilliance. The Rockies' batters fell victim to his throws one by one, their swings fading to whimpers in the face of his powerful arm.

The pressure started to increase in the third inning when Kershaw mustered an extra surge of energy-- his pitches taking on a miraculous quality. The crowd went wild when he hit out the side with powerful deliveries that seemed to cut through the air like blades of light.

In the fifth inning, a unique energy was felt through the crowd. The stakes were higher and history was calling. With a determined gaze, Kershaw continued his masterwork. He struck out batter after batter, a record-setting performance that etched his name in the record books.

With each successive strikeout, the crowd held its breath, sensing that something amazing was taking place. The tension reached a fever pitch and the atmosphere heated with anticipation. Kershaw, seemingly impervious to the pressure, displayed a calm poise.

By the ninth inning, Kershaw stood at the face of greatness. The stadium waited, every spectator's eyes locked on the mound. With each pitch, his arm propelled him closer to destiny, the exciting prospect of history within his grasp.

The last batter, a solitary figure against the pinnacle of pitching dominance, went into the box. The crowd stood up, their voices rising in a wave of confidence and hope. Kershaw's fingers curled around the ball and his focus sharpened as he prepared to throw.

The pitch was thrown--a wild curveball that was impossible to predict. The batter swung, but missed the ball completely. The sound of the ball breaking the catcher's mitt echoed around the stadium like a triumphant chime, marking the conclusion of a remarkable journey.

Clayton Kershaw had just thrown a no-hitter!

The crowd gave a standing ovation. Kershaw was quickly surrounded by his teammates, who showered him with a cacophony of praise.

On that night, Kershaw was able to break free from his mortal coil in a game that would go down in baseball history as a brilliantly executed achievement. The no-hitter was a monument to his unmatched talent and unwavering determination--cementing his spot as one of baseball's all-time great pitchers.

Chapter 13
A Multi-Homer for the Ages – Ken Griffey Jr

A s the sun began to set over Seattle's Kingdome on May 24, 1996, an orange glow spread over the ballpark. As the Seattle Mariners and the New York Yankees hit the field, the atmosphere was electric with the promise of a game that would go down in baseball lore. But on this night, it was Ken Griffey Jr. who stole the show.

Affectionately known as "The Kid," Griffey was a talented outfielder who wowed fans with his smooth moves on the field. The picture-perfect swing and prolific home runs made Griffey famous. In his legendary career, he made the All-Star team 13 times, won 10 Gold Gloves, and belted 630 home runs.

Beginning his baseball career at an early age, Griffey followed in the footsteps of his father, Ken Griffey Senior. Early on, Ken Griffey Jr. encountered several obstacles that tested his resilience and determination. Despite being selected first overall in the 1987 MLB Draft, Griffey Jr. faced skepticism and criticism regarding his ability to meet the enormous expectations set on him. Some critics questioned whether he could live up to the expectations and become the superstar that many anticipated. In addition, Griffey Jr. struggled with a number of injuries that temporarily hindered his performance on the field.

However, Ken Griffey Jr.'s exceptional talent and unwavering work ethic enabled him to overcome these obstacles and develop great abilities. He devoted himself to perfecting his hitting and fielding techniques, practicing tirelessly to better his swing and defensive prowess. Griffey Jr. incorporated fitness and strength training into his regimen, ensuring that he remained in peak physical condition to reduce the impact of injuries.

Griffey Jr.'s performances on the field demonstrated his desire to disprove his critics. He soon emerged as one of the game's premier power hitters after displaying remarkable hitting consistency.

Playing for the Seattle Mariners, Griffey Jr. had one of his most memorable games ever on May 24, 1996. The Seattle Mariners took the field against the legendary New York Yankees. The audience had no idea that they were about to witness a legendary performance that would forever be etched into the annals of baseball.

From the moment he strode onto the diamond, Ken Griffey Jr. exuded confidence and determination. As he settled into the batter's box with his eyes on the Yankees' pitcher, the stadium's commotion seemed to intensify. Griffey Jr. acknowledged the challenge before him and was eager to prove his valor against one of the game's most formidable opponents.

Early innings of the game were a tense back-and-forth with both teams fighting for the upper hand. However, Griffey Jr. made his first move in the fourth inning, the crack of his bat signifying the arrival of greatness. With one runner on base, he launched the ball into the night sky for a two-run home run that stunned Yankees fans and energized Mariners supporters.

As the game progressed, so did the aura of invincibility surrounding Griffey Jr. With the bases loaded in the sixth inning, he returned to the plate. The crowd held its breath as he swung with precision and unleashed a thunderous explosion that sent the ball soaring into the stands. Witnessing the sheer brilliance of one of baseball's brightest lights, the stadium shook with awe.

But Griffey Jr. was not yet finished. In the eighth inning, he took the final pitch as if destined to complete a masterpiece. All he needed to cement his legacy was a solo home run-- and with each swing, he defied gravity. And then it happened-- he struck the ball like a hammer, where it vanished into the night sky, the audience erupted in recognition of the moment's significance.

The Seattle Mariners celebrated a victory as the final out was recorded, but Ken Griffey Jr.'s historic performance persisted in the air. A feat for the ages, he had set a team record by scoring five runs in a single game. His four-for-four performance with a walk was flawless. However, it was the three home runs in a single game that displayed an exceptional show of strength and accuracy.

The legend of Ken Griffey Jr.'s extraordinary night spread throughout the baseball world in the days and years that followed. His performance that night at the Kingdome became a part of baseball lore, and his name aligned with excellence.

Chapter 14
The Catch That Made History – Willie Mays

The first game of the 1954 World Series pitted the New York Giants against the Cleveland Indians. The Polo Grounds in New York City came alive with excitement as the two teams took the field. There was a buzz of anticipation in the air since the fate of a championship was at stake.

With manager Leo Durocher at the helm, the Giants were focused on winning championships for San Francisco. Sal Maglie, the right-handed flamethrower, stepped onto the mound, ready to show off his pitching skills. As the game progressed, so did the anxiety. No team was able to break the stalemate as they traded blows without scoring. Each spectator's heartbeat mirrored the game's ups and downs as the crowd waited for the next play.

With two outs and the game tied 2-2, the Cleveland Indians came out swinging in the top of the eighth inning when Vic Wertz came to the plate. The crowd's collective breath became heavy with expectation of what was to come.

Maglie, concentrating deeply, threw a pitch that Wertz slammed with a thunderous crack. As the ball was hit, it soared high and deep towards center field. It looked like a lost cause for the Giants and their diehard fans, as it was headed straight towards the outfield fence.

However, a man suddenly came out of the darkness. Center fielder for the Giants, the lightning-fast Willie Mays, raced with an almost supernatural level of intensity. Mays ran toward the impending disaster, his eyes fixed on the falling ball, and time stood still.

Willie Mays had a legendary baseball career that spanned 22 seasons and earned him the reputation as one of the game's best players. His combination of speed, power hitting, and fielding prowess wowed spectators. Mays led the New York Giants to a victory at the 1954 World Series and was named National League MVP twice.

Willie Mays, who was born in Westfield, Alabama, on May 6, 1931, is largely considered to be among the sport's all-time greats. Mays made a lasting impression on baseball with his incredible athleticism, lightning-fast speed, and tremendous talents at the plate and in the outfield.

Mays' professional baseball career got off to a roaring start with the Birmingham Black Barons, when he displayed his extraordinary talent. Beginning a career that would last more than two decades, he debuted in the major leagues in 1951 with the New York Giants.

Mays had a tough time adjusting to major league baseball after making his debut, however. He was criticized for his poor batting performance and many strikeouts. Being one of the first African-American players in the National League brought additional pressure on Mays to perform well during a time of racial segregation in baseball.

Willie Mays overcame these early obstacles thanks to his tremendous talent and work ethic. He put in a lot of time and effort to get better both at bat and on the field. Mays meticulously worked to improve his hitting technique and pitch detection with the help of coaches and older players like mentor and teammate Monte Irvin. He put in work on defense as well, earning praise for his range and acrobatic catches as a center fielder.

Mays' remarkable talents immediately became a crowd-pleaser when he took the field. He was unlike anyone else of his era because of his extraordinary offensive and defensive abilities. Acrobatic catches like "The Catch" in the 1954 World Series, in which Mays made a spectacular over-the-shoulder grab while sprinting full speed, showcased Mays' outstanding fielding talents.

On that day, Mays performed the seemingly impossible as Vic Wertz's ball traveled into an unreachable plane for any outfielder. With each step, Mays got closer to the disappearing orb. The spectators knew the significance of the moment, so they all watched the dazzling display of athletic skill, holding their breath.

Mays, his torso at full extension, made a remarkable gesture by raising his gloved hand above his head. As he snatched the ball out of the jaws of despair, his fingertips touched the stars. As Mays defied gravity and the expectations of mere mortals by clutching the baseball, the crowd erupted in a tremendous roar of applause.

The grandeur of the event jolted the Polo Grounds to its very foundations, and the crowd went wild with celebration. The Giants' hopes for success were given new life thanks to the power and skill of one individual. Those who were fortunate enough to see the brilliance of "The Catch" will never forget it.

With renewed vigor and confidence thanks to Mays's heroics, the Giants took the field for the bottom of the eighth inning. The game went on, the stakes growing higher with each pitch, but the Giants, inspired by the idea that they could win if they just kept believing-- eventually did.

The Giants prevailed in the end, winning Game 1 on their way to a World Series championship. Mays' incredible catch had become a watershed moment, symbolic of the tenacity and determination that would define their championship run.

Baseball fans of all ages can look to "The Catch" as proof that exceptional things are possible through focus and physical prowess. There is no doubt that Willie Mays' brilliant play will always be remembered as one of the greatest moments in baseball history.

Chapter 15
A Power Hitter at Briggs Stadium – Hank Greenberg

T he baseball world was buzzing with excitement in the golden light of a late September afternoon in 1938. In a thrilling doubleheader against the great St. Louis Browns, one player was on the verge of etching his name into the books of history.

The stadium was packed, and the fans' anticipation of the game was contagious. Like a dense cloud, anxiety hung heavy in the ballpark.–Hank Greenberg stepped into the batter's box. His broad shoulders felt the weight of the situation, but he was unfazed.

Hank Greenberg made his mark in professional baseball throughout the 1930s and 1940s. He was born on January 1, 1911, in New York City. Greenberg was one of the most feared sluggers of his period-- his towering 6 feet 4 inches of height further added to his intimidating reputation.

Before making his debut with the Detroit Tigers in 1930, Greenberg played in the minor leagues, where he immediately rose to prominence, demonstrating his fearsome hitting skills. Greenberg's massive home runs and steady offensive made him a star right away.

Greenberg had some early success, but his career was met with adversity. Greenberg, a Jewish player in an era dominated by social discrimination, faced anti-Semitism from fans and opponents alike. Steadfast, he ignored the opposition and used his talents to outshine his detractors.

Greenberg overcame adversity because of his unyielding determination and commitment to enhancing his batting abilities. He had innate hitting skills and power, but he diligently practiced to improve his swing and plate discipline. Greenberg rapidly developed into a dangerous hitter thanks to his hard work in the cage and meticulous preparation. His remarkable power hitting (he hit over 40 home runs in multiple seasons) and ability to consistently drive in runs made him a household name.

Greenberg's breakout season came in 1934 when he hit an impressive .339 with 139 RBIs and 26 home runs. He continued to excel in subsequent seasons, becoming a key figure in the Tigers' lineup and a feared slugger throughout the league.

In 1938, Hank Greenberg had been chasing Babe Ruth's single-season home run record for weeks. On September 27, 1938 at Briggs Stadium, the air was packed with excitement as the first game of the doubleheader began. Tigers fans held their breath, hoping to witness something remarkable.

Greenberg approached the plate with a determined look in his eyes. As the pitcher wound up, delivering a fastball that seemed to blur through the air, the tension was apparent. Greenberg's bat then struck like a cannon blast, sending the ball soaring high into the sky.

As the ball soared over the outfield wall and into history, the crowd erupted in loud cheers. Hank Greenberg's swing tied Jimmie Foxx's American League record of 58 home runs in a single season. The stadium erupted in applause, recognizing the historic achievement.

A true testimonial to the game itself, the event was a spiritual high for the spectators. It was inevitable that the story of that game would be passed down from one generation to the next. The day Hank Greenberg rallied the Tigers to victory and made baseball history!

Chapter 16
A Warrior at Fenway – Pedro Martinez

On a brisk October night in 1999, as Fenway Park readied for one of baseball's most highly awaited matchups, the air crackled with excitement. In the American League Championship Series, archrivals the Boston Red Sox and the New York Yankees squared off.

Pedro Martinez, the Red Sox's top pitcher, took the mound as the sun dipped below the horizon. Each of the thousands of spectators in the stadium was focused on him, making his every action feel like it carried the aspirations of an entire city. Facing the Yankees' potent and tenacious lineup, he realized the challenge that lay ahead.

The first pitch was thrown, and the battle commenced...

Famous for his explosive fastball and lethal changeup, Pedro Martinez was a dominant and ferocious pitcher. Martinez has had a long and varied career, with positions with the Red Sox and the Mets among others. He was named to the All-Star team eight times and earned three Cy Young Awards while helping the Red Sox win the World Series in 2004 after an 86-year drought.

Martinez suffered with control concerns in his early years, which resulted in high walk rates and pitch inconsistency. However, Martinez's perseverance and resilience were critical in overcoming these obstacles and honing his pitching skills. He worked relentlessly on his mechanics and conditioning, transforming his frame into a source of power and deception on the pitch. Martinez worked hard to improve his control and command, which resulted in a unique ability to paint the corners of the strike zone with his devastating arsenal of pitches.

Pedro Martinez emerged into one of the most dominant pitchers in MLB history through rigorous work and dedication to his profession. During his peak years, his fastball, paired with a devastating changeup and nasty breaking balls, made him practically unhittable.

On October 16, 1999, Pedro Martinez pitched a legendary game for the Boston Red Sox against the New York Yankees-- a showdown between two legendary teams, where Pedro Martinez delivered a performance worthy of the history books.

At the start of the game, Martinez uncorked a blistering fastball that roared toward home plate, thanks to his smooth windup and fierce arm speed. The crowd held its breath as the first pitch landed solidly in the catcher's mitt, signaling the start of a high-stakes game of chess between the pitcher and the batter.

The tension built inning by inning, like a coiled spring. Martinez's pitching performance held the crowd spellbound. His wicked movement and perfect accuracy shocked even the most seasoned batters. The Yankees' powerful attack, often capable of unleashing havoc, was muzzled by Martinez's dominant throw.

After each strike out, the Red Sox fans exploded in the stands with cheers, their voices spreading across Fenway Park. Martinez appeared superhuman on the mound. Each throw, like a symphony of orchestrated mayhem, ratcheted up the tension and made the game unforgettable.

The Yankees saw their chance to claim their victory at the top of the seventh inning and staged a comeback. With the possibility of breaking the scoreless tie so close, their runners made it onto the bases.

But Martinez, ever the fierce competitor, delivered pitch after pitch with the fierce determination of a seasoned warrior. He threw a series of perfect pitches-- his fingertips unleashing a barrage of swinging strikes and foul tips.

Martinez used his final surge of energy to strike out the side, putting an end to the Yankees' aspirations of a victory. The frenzied cheering of the crowd was a testimonial to the grandeur they had just seen. Martinez soaked in the excitement of the crowd.

Even though the outcome was already decided, the game continued, but the spotlight was squarely on Martinez, who delivered plays that will go down as one of baseball's all-time greats. Those in attendance that October night at Fenway Park will never forget the moments they witnessed.

Chapter 17
A New Hitting Streak Record – Joe DiMaggio

On May 15, 1941, the stage was set for what would become one of baseball's most memorable days. Joe DiMaggio, the legendary outfielder for the New York Yankees, strode onto the field at Yankee Stadium with resolve in his eyes. Nobody expected that this seemingly regular spring afternoon would signal the start of an amazing journey.

Giuseppe Paolo DiMaggio, better known as "Joe DiMaggio," was born on November 25, 1914, in Martinez, California, and went on to become a legendary baseball player. Known as "The Yankee Clipper," he became a legend due to his unmatched talent, poise on the field, and groundbreaking accomplishments.

DiMaggio was born into a modest Italian-American household, and he began practicing baseball at a young age. The

New York Yankees saw potential in him right away, and he signed with the team in 1936, beginning a career that would go down in baseball history.

Joe DiMaggio endured challenges early in his career due to injuries and questions about his talents. Shortly after making his Major League debut with the New York Yankees in 1935, he suffered a knee injury that hampered his effectiveness and kept him out for the rest of the season. Furthermore, some critics questioned whether DiMaggio's unconventional swing could be effective at the highest level. Because of his swing mechanics, several speculated that he may struggle against elite pitchers.

Despite these early difficulties, Joe DiMaggio's dedication to improving his batting skills enabled him to overcome them. He worked hard with hitting coaches and teammates to improve his swing and plate approach. DiMaggio's hard ethic and dedication paid off, as he quickly exhibited incredible consistency and power as a hitter. His distinctive swing became linked with grace and effectiveness, propelling him to become one of baseball's most feared batters.

As DiMaggio's career proceeded, his on-field performance silenced his naysayers. The influence of DiMaggio was instantaneous. He showed off his immense talent in his first professional season by hitting .323 and playing outstanding defense in center field. At the plate, he was a threat because of his speed, quickness, and strong swing.

DiMaggio's popularity soared through the 1930s and 1940s. During his thirteen-year stint with the Yankees, he became the team's beating heart and inspired them to an unprecedented nine World Series titles. His fluid and graceful playing won him a reputation as one of the best all-around players of his day.

DiMaggio's greatest accomplishment was setting a record in 1941 that has not been broken since. Incredible consistency saw him get a hit in 56 straight games, breaking Wee Willie Keeler's record of 44 games. This record, popularly known as "The Streak," launched DiMaggio into the public eye and cemented his reputation as one of baseball's all-time greats.

One of the most memorable and amazing feats in baseball history is Joe DiMaggio's 56-game hitting streak from May 15 to July 16, 1941. Over the course of 56 consecutive games, "The Yankee Clipper" changed the face of baseball and captured the attention of the whole country.

The streak started on a breezy spring afternoon at Yankee Stadium on May 15, 1941. DiMaggio was at bat for the New York Yankees against the Chicago White Sox, and he was expected to carry the team's hopes on his shoulders. He lined the first ball he saw to left field for a base hit, and his swing looked effortless. Nobody could have predicted that this relatively harmless hit would set off a run that would win the hearts of millions.

DiMaggio's remarkable reliability at the plate was on full display in game after game. The hits just kept on coming, and the crowd's enthusiasm only rose as the days went on. Spectators flocked to the stadiums to witness history being made.

The media frenzy grew when the winning streak approached 20, 30, and beyond. Newspapers splashed headlines about DiMaggio's accomplishment, and radio commentators reported each hit with suspense and drama.

The stakes were raised with each game, but DiMaggio appeared to thrive on the attention. He handled himself with remarkable grace, refusing to let the gravity of the situation shake his demeanor. He was able to keep the streak alive by finding openings in the field with relative ease, regardless of whether he was throwing a fastball or a curveball.

All eyes and ears were on the streak when it reached the halfway point. Even though it began as a baseball narrative, it quickly became a symbol of optimism and inspiration in the months before the United States entered World War II.

DiMaggio broke Willie Keeler's record of 44 consecutive games on July 2, 1941 in front of a sold-out crowd at Cleveland's Municipal Stadium. An already remarkable accomplishment was given even more weight by the fact that it set a new record.

DiMaggio's hitting seemed unstoppable despite constant pressure from the other squad. Despite facing the league's top pitchers, he consistently found his way on base.

On July 16, 1941, the 56th game of the run, the record ended at the hands of the Cleveland Indians. However, DiMaggio's accomplishment was unrivaled even in loss. The hitting streak had enthralled the country and forever altered baseball.

Joe DiMaggio's 56-game hitting streak set a new standard for baseball that stood for many years. It's a credit to DiMaggio's exceptional skill, fortitude, and commitment to baseball that his record has stood the test of time. The Yankee Clipper will forever be remembered as a baseball icon thanks to his unbeatable hitting streak.

Chapter 18
A No-Hitter At Yankee Stadium – Jim Abbott

O n a cool September night in 1993, the scene was set at the legendary Yankee Stadium. The New York Yankees and Cleveland Indians were getting ready for a game that would end up shocking everyone. Nobody could have predicted that this would be the night when a pitcher named Jim Abbott defied the odds and wrote himself into baseball history.

The crowd was on the edge of its seat when Jim Abbott, who was born without a right hand, ascended the mound. Some people still had their doubts about his ability to compete with the Indians' powerful lineup. However, Abbott was driven by determination and an unbreakable will to prove his skeptics wrong.

Abbott was born on September 19, 1967, in Flint, Michigan, with phocomelia, a disorder that left him without a right hand. Rather than allowing his physical limitations to define him, Abbott was determined to pursue his love of baseball from a young age.

He polished his talents throughout his youth, demonstrating an incredible skill for the sport despite the hurdles he endured. His hard work and dedication paid off, as he was accepted to the prestigious University of Michigan, where he played college baseball for the Wolverines. Abbott's collegiate accomplishments were nothing short of outstanding, and his ability on the mound drew the attention of scouts from Major League Baseball teams. His journey from college to the professional league would become a stunning tribute to the strength of the human spirit and the power of endurance.

Jim Abbott's glove switching pitching technique was awe-inspiring and clever, allowing him to adequately field his position as a pitcher despite his missing right hand. Abbott would pitch while wearing a custom-made glove with an enlarged and specially crafted wristband. This wristband would wrap over his right wrist, locking the glove in place. Abbott would quickly switch the glove from his throwing hand (left hand) to his right forearm after delivering the pitch. This quick movement enabled him to field the ball with his bare left hand instantly after pitching.

Abbott's glove switching technique was honed over the years, allowing him to play defense as good as any other pitcher in the league. However, teams at all levels routinely bunted to him in an attempt to exploit his fielding disadvantage. Another obstacle Abbott had to combat was the distrust of scouts, coaches, and even fellow players who didn't believe he belonged at the professional level. He also had to deal with the constant scrutiny of the media and the public. However, Abbott was intent on proving his doubters wrong, and his diligence paid off as his incredible talent began to receive wider notice.

When Jim Abbott was pitching for the New York Yankees on September 4, 1993, he accomplished an incredible feat. As the Cleveland Indians were the visitors to New York City's Yankee Stadium, the audience held its breath as Abbott's left hand released the opening pitch. When the Indians' leadoff batter made contact, the ball rocketed into the outfield with a crack of the bat heard across the stadium. In response, Abbott showed off his incredible reflexes by diving to his right and snatching the ball out of the air with his glove—all to the shock and awe of the spectators.

Abbott suddenly seemed to reach a higher plane. For the rest of the game, his pitches danced over the strike zone with pinpoint accuracy, inning after inning. With each batter he struck out, Abbott was getting closer to a truly remarkable feat.

Abbott's resolve strengthened with each swing, his intensity remaining constant. He was a man with a mission: to forever cement his place in baseball lore.

When the top of the ninth inning rolled around, Abbott was on the verge of history. The stakes were extremely high as he was only three outs away from immortality. Everyone in the stadium held their breath as Abbott was ready to face the final two hitters. His resolve and composure were on full display throughout each and every pitch. Kenny Lofton of the Cleveland Indians came to bat, and with him went the team's last chance to end Abbott's no-hitter. However, Abbott's delivery was flawless as he threw a variety of fast-balls, curveballs, and changeups.

On a 3-2 count, Abbott threw a slider that broke low and outside for his final pitch.

After a swing and a miss by Lofton, Abbott and the Yankees completed the perfect game.

Abbott had struck out every batter!

Realizing the moment's importance, the fans let forth a thundering scream of shouts and ovation that resounded throughout the stadium.

Jim Abbott's no-hitter is celebrated as one of baseball's most moving moments. It's an illustration of what can be accomplished with hard work, determination, and the refusal to let one's physical condition restrict their dreams. Abbott's successes serves as an example to future generations that everything is possible so long as you put your heart and soul into it— but most importantly, have faith in yourself.

Chapter 19
An Offensive Glory – Albert Pujols

On a cool October night in 2011, as Game 3 of the World Series was set to take place at Rangers Ballpark in Arlington. The air was thick with anticipation. With the help of their enthusiastic home fans, the Texas Rangers had jumped out to a 2-0 series lead over the St. Louis Cardinals. The stars aligned for a baseball game that would go down in history books.

Without question, the Cardinals needed a spark to fire their ambitions of making a championship return, knowing full well the enormous challenge that was before them. They had no idea that Albert Pujols, their superstar, was about to deliver an out of this world performance.

Since his debut in 2001, Albert Pujols has been a major force in baseball due to his powerful hitting and consistent offensive performance. Pujols has amassed impressive career statistics, including over 3,000 hits and over 650 home runs, predominantly as a first baseman. He is a three-time Most Valuable Player, a 10-time All-Star, and a two-time World Series champion, with the St. Louis Cardinals and the Los Angeles Angels.

Early in his baseball career, Albert Pujols had major obstacles, mostly due to skepticism regarding his age and position. Concerns concerning the accuracy of his reported birth date cast doubt on his age and potential as a player when he was a young prospect from the Dominican Republic. His defensive qualities and his ability to establish a role on the field were also questioned by skeptics.

Nonetheless, Pujols' extraordinary ability and commitment were clear even in his early career. He swiftly silenced his critics by displaying his offensive prowess and all-around talent. Pujols devoted many hours to training, both at the plate and on defense, perfecting his swing and learning to play several positions. Because of his extraordinary hitting ability, power, and defensive abilities, he became an instant star in Major League Baseball.

As his career continued, Albert Pujols proved his doubters wrong and became one of baseball's all-time greats. He won three Most Valuable Player honors and set a record with almost 600 home runs.

Part of Pujols claim to victory came during Game 3 on October 22, 2011.

The nighttime sky bathed Arlington Ballpark, heralding the coming of a World Series showdown of epic proportions. On October 22, 2011, the Texas Rangers and the St. Louis Cardinals were getting ready for a crucial game—and Albert Pujols was about to make history.

The audience went wild as the game started. Pujols strode up to the plate, towering above his opponents. He focused intently on the pitcher, and the air was thick with tension. A blistering fastball meant for the corners was thrown first, but Pujols had other ideas. With a vicious swing, he sent the ball sailing into the night, and the crack of wood on leather reverberated around the stadium.

The crowd went wild when Pujols rounded third base after hitting his first home run of the game. But no one in the crowd realized that they were seeing a historic moment. Pujols showed no mercy in his next at-bat, slamming another fastball over the left field wall. As he circled the bases again, the spectators looked on in amazement.

Pujols's at bats had an unearthly quality about them. He exploded out of control. He faced a different pitcher in his third at-bat, but that didn't change the outcome. For the third time in the game, he hit the ball so hard that it went flying over the fence. The audience was stunned, having just seen a performance that will live on in legend.

Records began to fall as Pujols kept pounding away at every pitch. That night, he joined an elite group of players by collecting five hits in a game of the World Series. With his six RBI, he broke yet another record. His mere actions were like moving poetry, forever engraving his name into the record books.

The Cardinals breezed to a commanding victory in the final inning. Pujols was the night's clear victor, and his name will live on in baseball lore. Future generations will look back in awe at the night when Albert Pujols, a diamond titan, took center stage and inscribed his name in the stars—- a name synonymous with October glory.

Chapter 20
A Legend Scores Three Home Runs – Mickey Mantle

The sun had just dipped below the horizon, and its golden light was washing over the magnificent Yankee Stadium. On May 13, 1955, the New York Yankees faced off against the Detroit Tigers in a baseball showdown like no other. Fans had no idea they were going to see a performance of such excellence that would forever cement this game in the annals of sports legend.

Mickey Mantle, a young man with steel determination, was one of the players that day. The Yankees' top outfielder was a switch-hitter with a reputation for extraordinary power. The fans were on the edge of their seats as he came up to the plate, expecting something truly remarkable to happen.

One of baseball's most recognizable players, Mickey Mantle was born in Spavinaw, Oklahoma, on October 20, 1931. He was a switch-hitting behemoth and remarkable athlete for the New York Yankees for his whole 18-year career. When Mantle took the field, he was an unstoppable force thanks to his formidable combination of strength, speed, and grace. Three times named American League Most Valuable Player, he also hit 536 home runs and was instrumental in the Yankees' domination in the 1950s and 1960s.

Mickey Mantle suffered multiple setbacks due to injuries early in his career. During his debut season in 1951, he suffered a major knee injury while attempting to catch a fly ball, limiting his mobility and speed greatly. Despite this setback, Mantle's enormous talent and promise were clear, though some questioned if he would ever fully recover and reach his full potential as a player.

However, Mantle's tenacity and perseverance enabled him to overcome these challenges and enhance his skills to become one of baseball's most legendary players. He worked hard on his conditioning and rehabilitation, gradually recovering his speed and agility. Mantle also worked on his batting, perfecting his swing to utilize his immense power. His innate talent, along with his persistent work ethic, rapidly established him as a force at the plate.

Mickey Mantle's spectacular achievements on the field silenced his doubters as his career continued. This was evident at Yankee stadium on May 13, 1955 when his team faced the Tigers.

As the first pitch sped toward him, Mantle took a beautiful swing from the left side of the plate—where he made solid contact with the ball. The baseball soared into the sky with a crack of the bat, like a shooting star leaving a trail of stardust behind it. It flew far beyond the outfield fence, and Mantle rounded the bases with assurance in his stride. As the first of his three home runs that evening was recorded, the fans went wild.

However, Mickey Mantle still had more in him. Perhaps shaken by the show of power, the Tigers' pitcher looked for a method to rein in the Yankee slugger. But Mantle was a formidable opponent. Later in the game, Mantle switched to the right side of the plate and again smashed the ball with such force that it flew well over the outfield fence.

Mantle had already accomplished something very unusual by hitting two home runs in a game. As the sun set and cast lengthy shadows over the field, the Tigers' pitcher must have felt as though he were up against a legendary beast, a baseball demigod wielding a bat of thunder. The crowd was on its feet as Mantle encountered the pitcher again in the latter innings. The atmosphere was tense, but Mantle maintained his composure.

Again, he connected with the ball with a mighty swing, and like a master craftsman, he sent it soaring into the night sky. With his third home run of the game, hit from the other side of the plate, he became the first player in baseball history to hit three home runs in a single game.

There was a loud shout across the stadium as even the opponents' fans recognized the grandeur they had just witnessed.

That day, Mantle's performance was more than a showcase of his talents; it was proof of the mythic power baseball had to transform ordinary people into heroes.

Mickey Mantle's name resounded around the stadium as the final out was made and the Yankees sealed the victory. His three home runs from both sides of the plate were a sight to behold and will live on in the memory of those who were there to see them. The young man from Oklahoma had forever engraved his name into baseball lore, and his accomplishments would be spoken about with reverence for years to come.

Chapter 21
A Home Run Redemption – George Brett

On a steamy afternoon in July of 1983, the New York Yankees and the Kansas City Royals met at Yankee Stadium for a pivotal baseball game. Tensions ran high as two of baseball's most historic teams squared off, each gunning for the other's crown.

The Royals' legendary third baseman, George Brett, was up to bat as the game hung in the balance. There were two outs and a runner on third with the score knotted at 4-4 in the top of the ninth inning. The audience went silent as everyone knew the outcome of the next pitch would determine the game's outcome.

Born George Howard Brett in Glen Dale, West Virginia on May 15, 1953, George Brett was a MLB baseball player best known for his 21-year stint with the Kansas City Royals. He is considered by many to be among baseball's all-time greats at third base.

George Brett came from a very baseball-oriented household. His father, Jack Brett, was a minor leaguer, and both Ken and Bobby Brett followed in his footsteps by playing the sport professionally. George acquired his baseball talents at a young age and rapidly grew to love the game.

His excellent batting average and impressive power hitting made him a reliable offensive threat. Brett had one of the best seasons in Major League Baseball history in 1980, when he led the league with a .390 batting average, hit 24 home runs, and drove in 118 runs. He earned the first of three batting titles that season and was chosen MVP of the American League.

Throughout his amazing career, Brett won countless awards and recognition. He played third base with such excellence that he was recognized with 13 All-Star selections, three Silver Slugger Awards, and a Gold Glove Award. In 1985, he was named the Most Valuable Player of the World Series after helping lead the Royals to their first and only championship.

George Brett overcame several obstacles in his life and career, and these experiences influenced how he played the game of baseball. One of the challenges he faced was dealing with the intense scrutiny that comes with being such a gifted and public figure in the sport.

George Brett came from a baseball family, with both his father and two of his brothers having played professionally. There was a lot of pressure on him to succeed in the sport and live up to the name of his family. While most athletes would have caved under such scrutiny, Brett used it as fuel to push himself to his physical and mental limits.

Brett struggled at the beginning of his MLB career to adapt to the level of play. At the plate, he had trouble finding his rhythm in his first two seasons. Brett, though, showed perseverance and hard effort despite the setbacks. He continued to work hard to get better, and his efforts were rewarded when he began to play up to his potential as a batter.

Brett looked directly at Goose Gossage, the intimidating closer for the Yankees, and concentrated. Gossage wound up to throw a blistering fastball and the motion sent vibrations through the ground. Brett swung wildly and connected, producing a loud crack that could be heard all throughout the stadium. Over the right field fence, the ball sailed into the New York sky.

After what looked like a stunning go-ahead home run, the Royals' dugout and fans went into a frenzy of celebration. Brett's historic power display sent chills down the spines of the Yankees. The mood changed abruptly as he passed home plate and headed back to the dugout, from elation to perplexity.

Billy Martin, manager of the Yankees, came out of the dugout, his face twisted in wrath. His voice boomed with accusation as he pointed at Brett's bat. The Yankees had seen that Brett's bat had an illegal amount of pine tar on it.

The umpires discussed the situation and came to a surprising conclusion after some lengthy deliberation. Brett's home run was thrown out and he got called out for using a prohibited bat. Brett was infuriated by the wave of disbelief that engulfed the crowd. His teammates tried to calm him down, but his feelings were too strong, and he exploded in rage.

In a shocking turn of events, Royals manager Dick Howser formally appealed the decision to the league office. Everyone in baseball was waiting for the verdict with eagerness.

A few days later, the commissioner's office released their decision, and the baseball world waited anxiously once more. The league sided with the Royals. The contested home run by Brett was ruled a home run, and play was restarted from that point.

George Brett had not only redeemed himself, but also inscribed his name into the baseball record books. The Pine Tar Game became a moment in baseball history-- a story of tenacity and resolve in the face of adversity.

George Brett's status as one of baseball's all-time greats was cemented as his legend and the Pine Tar Game grew with the passing of time. His legacy was defined not only by his extraordinary aptitude, but also by his ability to overcome adversity and triumph over seemingly insurmountable obstacles. It was a moment that encapsulated the essence of baseball — a game characterized by passion, emotion, and the relentless pursuit of greatness.

Chapter 22
The Yankee's Mr. October – Reggie Jackson

On the evening of October 18, 1977, New York City experienced a cool, fresh autumn evening. As the New York Yankees prepared to face their bitter rivals, the Los Angeles Dodgers, in Game 6 of the World Series, the legendary Yankee Stadium hummed with anticipation. This was the moment Reggie Jackson had been waiting for, his chance to shine on the biggest stage of them all.

Reggie Jackson, born Reginald Martinez Jackson on May 18, 1946, in Abington, Pennsylvania, is a former professional baseball player and one of Major League Baseball's most recognizable people. Jackson's impact on the game stretched beyond the field, as he became a trailblazer for African-American athletes in the sport. He was nicknamed "Mr. October" for his legendary postseason heroics.

Reggie Jackson grew up in a working-class neighborhood in Pennsylvania, where he developed an early interest in baseball. He went to Cheltenham High School, where his excellent baseball talents began to draw attention. He was a standout high school player, displaying talent as both a pitcher and an outfielder.

Jackson's outstanding high school performance won him a scholarship to Arizona State University to play collegiate baseball. As a student-athlete, he continued to flourish, and his talent drew the attention of MLB scouts. The Kansas City Athletics selected him as the second overall pick in the 1966 MLB Draft.

Jackson made his Major League Baseball debut with the Kansas City Athletics in 1967 and then joined the Oakland Athletics once the team relocated. He rapidly became recognized for his extraordinary power hitting, with huge home runs that seemed to defy gravity. Jackson's magnetic charm and flair for the dramatic helped him become a fan favorite.

Reggie Jackson's influence on baseball transcends his on-field accomplishments. As one of the first African-American players to achieve superstar status, he broke down racial barriers and served as a role model for innumerable black athletes in training. His charisma and leadership contributed to the sport's increased prominence, establishing him as a transcendent figure in baseball.

Jackson confronted immense pressure to live up to the lofty expectations placed on him at a young age, when he was a highly touted prospect. After being drafted by the Kansas City Athletics with the second overall selection in 1966, he advanced rapidly to the major leagues but initially struggled to find his footing. Fans and the media equally criticized and doubted him, which could have easily deterred a less determined player. Jackson used these early difficulties as motivation to work harder, hone his abilities, and demonstrate his worth as a top-tier player.

During his early years in the league in the 1960s and 1970s, Reggie Jackson was one of the few African-American players. On and off the field, he was subjected to racial prejudice and confronted with difficult circumstances. However, Jackson demonstrated remarkable resilience and determination, refusing to let such adversity affect his performance. He advocated for change and paved the way for future generations of African-American athletes.

There was a lot riding on Jackson's performance in Game 6 of the 1977 World Series against the Los Angeles Dodgers. Instead of crumbling under the spotlight, Jackson embraced it, belting up three home runs that single-handedly won the game for the Yankees. With this feat, he became an instant icon in baseball history.

Reggie Jackson's game was heavily influenced by his resilience and ability to succeed in high-stakes situations. He channeled his adversity into a drive for success, using it to push him forward and learn from his setbacks. Jackson's tenacity, work ethic, and unyielding confidence not only led to on-field success and acclaim, but also to his status as a groundbreaking baseball icon. The impact that tenacity and determination can have on a player's career and life is epitomized by his history as a powerful and prominent player.

The crowd was pumped up and ready to go when the Yankees hit the field. The grounds were set for a free-for-all showdown, and the atmosphere was electric with anxiety. As Jackson went into the batter's box, he could feel the pressure of the world watching him. The game was deadlocked, and the winner would decide the season.

Reggie squared off against Burt Hooton, the Dodgers' top pitcher and a difficult opponent known for his clever deliveries, as the audience cheered wildly. Now that there were two people in scoring position, everything was on the line.

Hooton threw a fireball, but Jackson was as alert as an eagle. He unleashed a magnificent swing that sent the ball deep into the New York night. The fans went wild as the ball sailed over the fence in right field for a three-run home run. The crowd of loyal Yankees knew they had seen a performance that would live long in their minds.

However, Reggie Jackson was not finished. Elias Sosa, a Dodgers reliever, was the opponent in his next at-bat. Jackson displayed steely nerves once again as he waited for the perfect pitch. Jackson's quick reactions and good vision allowed him to avoid the slider that Sosa threw. The ball was hit with such force that it soared into the night sky and was lost to the New York gloom. After another home run, the crowd erupted in joyous excitement.

Reggie Jackson strode toward the plate for the third time, as possessed by some unseen force. Once combative, the Dodgers now appeared both defeated and in awe of Jackson's genius.

Sosa threw a fastball at Jackson, who made an effortless swing-- the ball left the bat like a comet hurtling into the night sky. The crowd held its collective breath as Jackson hit his third home run, but the ball easily went over the fence.

The climax was attained when the Stadium erupted in a cacophony of cheers, applause, and "Reggie! Reggie!" chants. Jackson's unprecedented feat of hitting three home runs in a single World Series game cemented his place in baseball history.

Reggie Jackson's performance in Game 6 became legendary. That night, his bat had transformed into a mystical wand, painting the sky with triumphant symphonies. As the Yankees won the World Series, Reggie had permanently inscribed his name into the annals of baseball history.

From that point forward, Reggie Jackson would be known eternally as "Mr. October." His legacy would endure, motivating generations of baseball players to embrace the pressure, grasp the moment, and perform at their absolute best when it mattered most. In the tapestry of baseball's illustrious history, Reggie Jackson's masterwork would endure as a symphony of triumph, echoing through time as a reminder of the enchantment that can occur under the October lights.

Chapter 23
A Season Record at Shibe Park – Ted Williams

When the sun finally went down, throwing a golden glow across Shibe Park on September 28, 1941, the audience went silent in anticipation. Williams strode up to the plate, his eyes bright with concentration. The air was thick; everyone present understood the gravity of the situation. In his last at-bat, Williams needed to reach base to hit .400, a record where he would hit over 40% of his at-bats for the season. This record had not been achieved in over a decade.

Theodore Samuel "Ted" Williams was born in San Diego, California on August 30, 1918, and went on to become a legendary baseball player. Williams, widely recognized as one of the best hitters of all time, is universally hailed for his extraordinary talent at the plate and unwavering commitment to baseball.

Ted Williams was born and raised in San Diego, California, where he discovered baseball at a young age and dedicated the rest of his life to it. He spent many hours as a kid perfecting his swing, often in improvised batting cages he set up in the backyard. Even at a young age, Williams' extraordinary potential was visible, and it was clear that he possessed that uncommon combination of natural talent and relentless perseverance.

Williams's talents were noted, and the Boston Red Sox signed him as a free agent amateur baseball player in 1936. On April 20, 1939, he debuted in Major League Baseball and immediately became a hitter's hitter. Williams became famous for his hitting prowess due to his amazing vision, quick reflexes, and tremendous strength. His ability to analyze pitches was unmatched, and his swing was so flawless that he became known as "The Splendid Splinter."

Ted Williams overcame many obstacles in his life and baseball career, and these experiences shaped his outlook on the game and his unrivaled commitment to hitting. Early in his career, some coaches and scouts doubted Ted Williams' talent as a young player due to his unconventional approach to the plate. Williams, though, never wavered in his self-confidence, and he spent many hours perfecting his swing and enhancing his striking talents. He took the negative feedback as inspiration to improve his game, and he ended up as one of the best hitters ever.

After his impressive start in the minors, Williams was met with sky-high hopes from Red Sox fans when he debuted in the majors. With nicknames like "The Kid" and "The Splendid Splinter" , Williams was expected to perform at a world-class level at all times. While most athletes would have buckled under the pressure of such high expectations, Williams excelled in the spotlight. He took the task head on, becoming very focused on his work and even lingering after games to study pitchers.

Over the course of his distinguished career, Williams garnered numerous awards and honors. Both in 1942 and 1947 he won the Triple Crown-- having the highest batting average, most home runs, and most RBIs. One of baseball's most elusive marks, his .406 average he was about to achieve in 1941 made him the last player to hit .400 in a full season.

In 1941, the Boston Red Sox were gearing up to take on the Philadelphia Athletics at Shibe Park, and the entire baseball world was buzzing with anticipation. Ted Williams, or "The Splendid Splinter," was on the verge of an unprecedented feat on this day: a. 400 batting average.

The crowd was on the edge of their seats with each pitch, turning each swing of the bat into an orchestra of tension. There was a heavy sense of excitement in the stadium as fans prepared to witness history.

The tension peaked during a two-ball, one-strike count. Fred Caligiuri, the pitcher, wound up and unleashed a fastball that hung in the air for what felt like an eternity. Williams's mind was a source of concentration, and his eyes never left the ball. He connected with the ball with ease and strength, sending it soaring into the Philadelphia sky.

The stadium erupted in a deafening shout as the ball landed safely, just beyond the outfielder's reach. Williams dashed to first base, the audience erupting in applause, clapping, and screaming his name. He'd done it - he'd hit .400, a feat accomplished by only a few players in the game's history.

Williams raised his cap to the adoring audience as he stood on first base, a satisfied smile on his face. His path to .400 had been difficult, with many ups and downs, but he had endured with unrivaled determination and skill. In that moment, he became a symbol of baseball perfection, a hitting master, and a hero to baseball fans all around the world.

The news of Williams' performance spread like wildfire, and the baseball world applauded this amazing player's accomplishment. His teammates, coaches, and fans all praised him, recognizing the significance of what he had accomplished.

Ted Williams' .406 batting average game in 1941 is considered one of the finest accomplishments in baseball history. His perfect season became legend, a timeless story of ability, perseverance, and the quest of greatness. Williams remained a hitting virtuoso throughout his storied career, dazzling spectators with his swing and unwavering commitment to perfection. His legacy as "The Splendid Splinter" lives on as an everlasting reminder of the beauty that may happen on a baseball diamond.

Chapter 24
A Record Home Run Streak – Don Mattingly

D on Mattingly took the field with an unwavering resolve in the summer of 1987. He was in the midst of a fantastic season, and rumors were circulating that he would set a new record.

Former MLB player and current manager Don Mattingly was born Donald Arthur Mattingly on April 20, 1961, in Evansville, Indiana. Mattingly, who played for the New York Yankees and is fondly known as "Donnie Baseball," is a baseball legend for his incredible talent and leadership on the field.

Don Mattingly loved baseball ever since he was a kid. While at Reitz Memorial High School, he participated in and excelled at a number of sports. Scouts took notice of his baseball skills, and the New York Yankees picked him up in the 19th round of the 1979 Major League Baseball Draft.

Mattingly opted to play college baseball for Indiana State University rather than join the Yankees organization right away. He received acclaim for his outstanding hitting ability during his collegiate career. He made All-America in 1980.

On September 8, 1982, Don Mattingly debuted with the New York Yankees of Major League Baseball. He was a first baseman with a Gold Glove reputation for his clean swing and outstanding leadership on and off the field. Mattingly's doggedness and commitment won him the affection of New Yorkers, who began calling him "Donnie Baseball."

Mattingly established himself as one of the game's top hitters during the 1980s and early 1990s. He won the American League Batting Title in 1984 with a .343 average and repeated the feat in 1985 with a .324 average.

Mattingly's most memorable season occurred in 1985, when he was selected the American League MVP. He led the league in hits, doubles, and RBIs that season, showcasing his all-around prowess as a player.

Despite his individual success, Mattingly's career was marred by the Yankees' inability to attain team success, and he never made it to the postseason. Nonetheless, his contributions to the team and constantly exceptional performance cemented his place as one of the most adored figures in Yankees history.

Don Mattingly struggled with doubt and uncertainty about his talents as a ballplayer in his early years. He was drafted late in the year, thus he had to work harder than more highly touted talents in the minor leagues to earn a spot with the New York Yankees. Early adversity spurred Mattingly's burning ambition and established in him the tenacious work ethic that would become a signature of his professional baseball career.

Don Mattingly's career as a player was jeopardized by injury. In 1987, he sustained a significant back injury that led to chronic pain and required surgery and months of rehabilitation. Mattingly, however, did everything in his power to get back on the field after suffering these setbacks. He proved his commitment to the sport and his ability to bounce back from setbacks by playing through a series of injuries and maintaining a high level of performance.

Mattingly was one of the league's top performers year in and year out, but the New York Yankees often struggled during his time there. Mattingly never got to show off his skills on baseball's biggest stage because his team never made the playoffs during his time there. Mattingly was admired by both his teammates and the fans despite the fact that he handled the setback in a professional manner and served as a leader within the club.

During the sweltering summer of 1987, the baseball world experienced an event that stunned both fans and players. It all started on a memorable July 8th evening when the New York Yankees faced the Minnesota Twins at Yankee Stadium.

Don Mattingly, a force to be reckoned with at the plate, entered the batter's box with a determined demeanor. He sent not one, but two baseballs soaring over the outfield wall with a crack of his bat—a historic performance that enthralled the crowd and set the setting for an unprecedented streak.

The tale continued the next day, on July 9th, when Mattingly played the Chicago White Sox. True to style, he produced another powerful swing, sending the ball soaring into the stands for his third home run in three games.

Mattingly's bat remained fire, as though propelled by an alien force. On July 10th, he swung with precision against the same White Sox, adding another home run to his increasing streak.

The Chicago White Sox must have felt like mere bystanders in the face of Mattingly's might the next day, July 11th. He hit another home drive into the stands, overcoming the odds and leaving the audience speechless.

Mattingly appeared unstoppable with each passing game. On July 12th, he gathered his extraordinary strength once more against the White Sox, sending another baseball over the distance.

Mattingly's determined pursuit of history resumed on July 16th, when the Yankees met the Texas Rangers at Arlington Stadium. He hit two more home runs with an aura of invincibility in a game that cemented his status as a baseball deity.

The streak wasn't done yet. Mattingly walked up to the plate again on July 17th, this time against the same Rangers, unmoved by the pressure and expectation. He smashed another home run, extending his fascinating streak, with a stroke that appeared to transcend time.

Finally, on a scorching July 18th afternoon, the crescendo reached a climax as the Yankees faced the Rangers again. Mattingly, the man with the Midas touch, hit one more home run to end his record-breaking streak of eight straight games with a home run.

The baseball world erupted in celebration and admiration, and the record books were rewritten in Don Mattingly's honor. His awe-inspiring performance had left an indelible impact on the hearts of fans all around the world, and his name would be murmured in reverence and awe for the rest of time. A legend was born in the hot summer of 1987, and Don Mattingly had sealed his spot as one of baseball's eternal heroes.

Chapter 25
The Stolen Base King – Rickey Henderson

At the Oakland-Alameda County Coliseum, the Oakland Athletics were hosting the New York Yankees for a regular season baseball game. Even before the first pitch was thrown, everyone in attendance knew that Rickey Henderson was on the verge of making history.

Rickey Henderson, born Rickey Henley Henderson in Chicago, Illinois on December 25, 1958, is a former professional baseball player and one of the most electrifying personalities in Major League Baseball history. Henderson, renowned for his lightning-fast speed, record-setting stolen base totals, and remarkable longevity, left an indelible mark on the sport and remains one of the greatest hitters and baserunners in the game.

Rickey Henderson's fascination with baseball began at a young age. He attended Oakland Technical High School while he was growing up in Oakland, California. There, evaluators and college recruiters began to take notice of his prodigious baseball abilities, which drew their attention.

Henderson's exceptional speed and athleticism earned him a baseball scholarship at the adjacent Oakland City College. He was drafted by the Oakland Athletics in the fourth round of the 1976 MLB Draft after impressing MLB organizations with his performance in college.

On June 24, 1979, Rickey Henderson made his Major League Baseball debut with the Oakland Athletics and immediately established himself as a force to be reckoned with. He acquired a reputation as one of the most feared leadoff hitters in the league due to his extraordinary speed on the bases.

Henderson grew up in a rough community in Oakland, California, and he struggled financially as a child. His family's limited means taught him the importance of hard labor and perseverance. Knowing that success in baseball could provide him and his family with a better existence, the adversity he faced as a youth fueled his desire to achieve baseball greatness.

Despite his extraordinary speed, some critics and baseball insiders were skeptical of Henderson. Some believed that his style of play, which relied largely on speed and baserunning, would not translate to sustained success in the majors.

Henderson used this uncertainty as motivation to disprove his detractors' claims. He concentrated on developing his abilities, increasing his batting average, and becoming a more well-rounded player.

As Henderson's career spanned more than two decades, he confronted the difficulty of adapting to changing baseball trends and the game's evolution. As he aged, his speed inevitably diminished, and he had to modify his strategy on the field in order to remain effective. Instead of solely relying on stolen bases, Henderson became more disciplined at the plate, drawing walks and utilizing his baseball IQ to capitalize on opponents' errors. He demonstrated his versatility and ability to contribute in various ways by becoming an all-around athlete.

Henderson's greatest achievement was passing Lou Brock as Major League Baseball's all-time leader in stolen bases on May 1, 1991. Henderson's 1,406 career stolen bases are a tribute to his speed and base-stealing prowess and remain one of baseball's most untouchable records to this day.

Henderson, one of baseball's most electrifying players, displayed his incredible speed and baserunning prowess throughout the game. Fans were on the edge of their seats every time he stepped onto the basepaths, waiting for him to finally make history.

The time had come in the fourth inning. Henderson, with the Athletics down by one, was poised to begin his quest for history at first base. Henderson, known for his lightning-fast base-stealing abilities, sprinted off first base as the pitcher threw the following pitch.

As the dust settled and the crowd cheered, it was official: Rickey Henderson had stolen his 939th base, passing Lou Brock's long-held record.

When Henderson's accomplishment was displayed on the scoreboard, the Oakland audience erupted in thunderous cheers. Fans and players alike stopped the game for a moment to applaud Henderson's historic achievement. The Yankees players clapped along, recognizing the grandeur of the player they had just seen.

The historic performance by Rickey Henderson on May 1, 1991, exemplified his extraordinary speed, baserunning skill, and influence on baseball. His record-breaking performance cemented his status as Major League Baseball's all-time best base thief.

Beyond the record, the game represented the incredible career of a player who personified thrill, mastery, and passion for the sport. Rickey Henderson's influence on baseball went well beyond the field of play, as he is still a revered figure today for his legendary accomplishments and electrifying on-field persona. Baseball fans all across the world take inspiration and fascination from his 939 career steals and his status as one of the game's all-time greats.

Chapter 26
A Play for the History Books – Stan Musial

On a sunny day in May, Busch Stadium in St. Louis, Missouri, was packed with excited spectators. The St. Louis Cardinals and the New York Giants were ready to play a doubleheader and it was sure to be a thrilling day of baseball. Yet still, they had no idea that they were about to witness a historic performance.

There was an electric atmosphere before the first game. Cardinals icon and outfielder Stan Musial took the field with laser focus. As the pitcher cranked, the crowd heard the snap of Musial's bat as he sent the ball sailing over the outfield fence.

The renowned baseball player Stan Musial, or "Stan the Man," as he was sometimes referred, will forever be remembered for the impact he had on the game. Born in Donora, Pennsylvania, USA on November 21st, 1920, Musial is a legendary player for the St. Louis Cardinals and widely regarded as one of the best hitters in MLB history.

Musial made his Major League Baseball debut on September 17, 1941, after signing with the St. Louis Cardinals in 1938. During the 1940s and 1950s, he was an integral part of the Cardinals' success and rapidly became a fan favorite.

Musial, a left-handed hitter and outfielder, was recognized for his fluid swing, high hitting average, and amazing consistency at the plate. He won seven batting titles in the National League and concluded his career with a lifetime hitting average of .331. Musial's all-around offensive style was complemented by his strong fielding and intuition.

Stan Musial had numerous hurdles during his baseball career, but his persistent passion and strong work ethic helped him to overcome them and become one of the game's greatest players. At the start of his career, Musial had to adjust to a position change when arm problems hampered his pitching talents. As a rookie player in the Major Leagues, he also faced the challenging job of adjusting to the increased level of competition and pressure. Musial's great work ethic and desire to progress, on the other hand, enabled him to swiftly find his footing and prosper in the major leagues.

His baseball career was temporarily cut short when he served in the United States Navy during World War II, but he maintained his focus and training during his military service, allowing him to return to baseball successfully after the war. Musial's mental resilience and poise allowed him to battle through difficult moments and restore top form even during severe slumps. Despite personal misfortunes, such as his father's death during his rookie season, Musial used baseball as an outlet for grief and continued to produce at an exceptional level. Balancing the demands of a baseball career and a family life could have been difficult, but Musial's strong family support system and priority of his loved ones allowed him to find balance in both facets of his life. His devotion to the game, his team, and his never-ending quest for progress cemented his legendary position both on and off the field.

On May 2, 1954, at Busch Stadium, baseball fans were treated to a truly extraordinary performance by Musial. The St. Louis Cardinals were playing the New York Giants, and the stage was set for a spectacular matchup between the two powerful teams.

The air was thick with excitement as the game began. Musial, noted for his graceful swing and exceptional hitting skills, took the plate in the first inning. The Cardinals' fans anxiously awaited Musial's signature brilliance.

Musial's bat met the fastball delivered by the pitcher with a perfect blend of power and precision. The crack of the bat rang around the stadium as the baseball flew high into the distance, going over the outfield wall for a thunderous home run. The audience erupted in applause as Musial circled the bases with ease, his first home run of the day now engraved in the scorebook.

But Musial wasn't finished yet. In the third inning, he approached the plate with renewed zeal. This time, the Giants' pitcher tried to fool him with a mix of breaking balls and off-speed offerings, but Musial was in his element. He connected with another pitch and sent it crashing into the seats, displaying an incredible ability to read pitches.

The audience was in awe as they witnessed the amazing performance develop before their eyes. Musial's hitting skill was on full display, leaving no doubt that they were watching a once-in-a-lifetime talent at his very finest.

Musial's confidence skyrocketed after hitting two home runs, and his every action seemed to exude inevitability. Even the Giants' players, who were no strangers to elite competition, couldn't help but marvel at the spectacle. Musial's effect grew beyond his home runs as the game progressed. His presence at the plate and on the field commanded respect, and the Giants found themselves up against a formidable opponent they couldn't contain.

Musial's performance that day was immortalized when the final out was recorded. Two home runs in a single game demonstrated his unequaled talent and ability to rise to the occasion when it mattered most.

Chapter 27
A Relentless Pitcher Who Broke Barriers – Satchel Paige

The stadium's crackling buzz rang through the air, heralding the entrance of a renowned figure - Satchel Paige. He stood tall on the pitcher's mound at 50 years old, his lean frame defying time.

The stadium was packed, a sea of faces hoping to catch a glimpse of the throwing maestro. Satchel inhaled deeply, the weight of a lifetime of baseball memories resting on his shoulders. He could feel the eyes on him, analyzing his every move. Satchel began his wind-up with a confident smile, the ball securely clutched in his hand. As he brought his arm forward, he delivered his characteristic pitch that sent shivers down batters' spines.

Satchel Paige, born Leroy Robert Paige on July 7, 1906, in Mobile, Alabama, was a great African-American baseball pitcher and one of the sport's most influential players. He is regarded as one of the best pitchers of all time, despite the fact that he spent much of his prime playing years in the segregated leagues owing to racial obstacles in Major League Baseball.

Paige got the nickname "Satchel" as a child because he used to carry bags and satchels at the train station to earn money. In the 1920s, he began his baseball career by playing for local semi-professional and industrial league teams. By the mid-1920s, he had joined the Southern League's Chattanooga Black Lookouts, where he established himself as a strong pitcher with a blazing fastball and a range of deceptive pitches.

Satchel Paige encountered various obstacles during his baseball career, many of them were directly tied to the racial segregation and discrimination that existed at the time. These difficulties included being denied entry into Major League Baseball, forcing him to play primarily in the segregated leagues and barnstorming exhibition games— which were games played outside of regular season. Despite these limits, Paige's performance and success in these games helped to challenge the perception that black players were inferior, eventually contributing to the color barrier being broken. He also had to deal with financial difficulties, earning lesser wages than white players and having to play in various leagues and on barnstorming tours to support himself. Despite the difficulties, Paige's inventiveness and adaptability on the field strengthened his playing style and flair.

Paige also had to deal with the difficulty of maintaining peak physical and mental condition for an extended period of time. His career extended five decades, and he performed well into his fifties. Nonetheless, his attention to conditioning and knowledge of the game allowed him to adapt his pitching technique as he aged, depending on precision and control rather than raw power. Travel and hotel issues were also prominent in the segregated leagues, with Paige having to endure long bus rides and poor lodging conditions when on the road. These adversities developed his perseverance and adaptability, which contributed to his ability to thrive in difficult situations on the field.

Furthermore, Paige's celebrity as one of the most prominent black athletes of his generation subjected him to continual attention, racial discrimination, and heightened criticism. He was able to maintain his cool and confidence, though, by viewing these problems as opportunities to constantly develop and prove his worth. Overcoming these challenges boosted Satchel Paige's game in a variety of ways. Playing in the segregated leagues and on barnstorming tours allowed him to build a strong arsenal of pitches, including a fastball, curveball, slider, and changeup. His mental toughness and adaptability allowed him to remain calm under duress and modify his techniques in response to opponents.

Paige's signing with the Cleveland Indians was a watershed moment in baseball history since it signaled the end of the American League's color barrier. He'd spent the majority of his famous career in the segregated leagues, displaying his amazing talent and talents to adoring black fans. However, due to the racial segregation that existed in professional baseball at the time, he was unable to play at the top level in the majors.

Bill Veeck, the owner of the Cleveland Indians, is recognized for his progressive views on race and a desire to win. Paige's debut drew a lot of media attention and fan excitement. On that momentous day, approximately 72,000 fans packed Cleveland's Municipal Stadium to witness his debut, demonstrating his enormous popularity and the significance of the occasion.

Paige entered the game as a relief pitcher in the fifth inning against the St. Louis Browns. Despite his age, he displayed tremendous pitching ability and control on the mound. The audience watched his legendary hesitation pitch, in which he would wait slightly during his wind-up, throwing batters off-balance and guessing.

Paige's performance in that game was outstanding, as he pitched three scoreless innings while allowing only one hit and clinching the Cleveland Indians' victory. His successful debut as a Major League pitcher at an age considered past most players' prime, combined with the breaking down of the color barrier in the American League, made this moment a historic and groundbreaking event in baseball history.

Satchel Paige's big league debut not only demonstrated his talent and skill, but it also paved the path for future African-American players to follow in his footsteps. It was a crucial step toward eventual baseball integration and led to the breaking down of racial boundaries in the sport. As a result, his debut remains one of the most notable and influential moments in Satchel Paige's incredible career.

Paige made history on July 9, 1948, when he took the mound for the Cleveland Indians, becoming the oldest rookie to ever play in the major leagues. Satchel Paige's debut in Major League Baseball at the age of 42 is regarded as a significant and legendary moment in his career.

In 1971, Satchel Paige was the first player from the African-American Leagues to be inducted into the Baseball Hall of Fame. He remained active in baseball as a coach and ambassador until his death on June 8, 1982, in Kansas City, Missouri.

Satchel Paige's contribution to baseball and legacy as a role model for African-American athletes cannot be understated-- his exceptional talent, charisma, and endurance in the face of racial hardship continue to inspire future generations of players and fans.

Chapter 28
A Hitting Marvel at Sportsman's Park – Ty Cobb

On a crisp spring afternoon in 1925, a calm wave of anticipation crept over Sportsman's Park in St. Louis, Missouri. The Detroit Tigers were in town to play the St. Louis Browns, and among the Tigers' lineup was the renowned Ty Cobb - a man whose name alone terrified opposing pitchers.

Tyrus Raymond Cobb, better known as Ty Cobb, was born on December 18, 1886, in Narrows, Georgia, USA. He is largely considered to be one of the greatest baseball players in Major League history. Cobb was a talented outfielder well-known for his fierce competitiveness, aggressive playing style, and incredible hitting talents.

Cobb made his MLB debut in 1905 with the Detroit Tigers and rapidly rose to prominence. He played for the Tigers for the majority of his career, from 1905 to 1926. Cobb retired after a 24-year career that included brief spells with the Philadelphia Athletics in 1927 and the Detroit Tigers (again) in 1928.

Ty Cobb, one of baseball's all-time greats, experienced various challenges throughout his remarkable career, but his intense dedication and perseverance allowed him to overcome each and continue to enhance his game. Cobb struggled as a young player to adjust to professional baseball, as his great competitiveness occasionally led to clashes with teammates and opponents. However, he saw the importance of channeling his energy productively and worked on improving his gaming strategy. Transitioning from the minors to the majors presented another obstacle, as he had to adjust to the increased level of competition and various skill sets of MLB pitchers. Nonetheless, he worked hard to perfect his hitting technique and study each pitcher's patterns, eventually becoming one of baseball's most effective hitters.

Cobb's unwavering work ethic led him to play through ailments, demonstrating his dedication and commitment to the game. He knew the need of staying in peak physical shape and never let setbacks derail his efforts. Cobb utilized hardship as fuel to exhibit his ability on the field and quiet his critics, despite facing prejudice and hostility from fans, opponents, and the media. He redirected his energy into becoming one of the game's most dominant players, transforming negativity into motivation.

Cobb set countless records and accomplished many awards during his career. Cobb won the American League hitting title 12 times and finished his career with the highest career batting average in MLB history—scoring a .366.

Cobb's aggressive playing style frequently resulted in on-field squabbles and altercations with both opponents and teammates. Despite this, his baseball talent was evident, and he established a reputation as one of the game's most intense rivals.

On May 5, 1925, the Detroit Tigers played the St. Louis Browns at Sportsman's Park. On that day, Ty Cobb's power-hitting abilities were on full display.

In the first inning, Cobb's steely gaze focused upon the ball with unflinching intent as the first pitch flew towards the plate. Crack! As Cobb sent the ball soaring over the outfield fence, the audience exploded in applause.

But that was just the start of the show that was about to begin. Cobb moved into the batter's box for his second at-bat with renewed passion. The pitcher delivered his offering, apprehensive of the powerful hitter looming before him. Whack! The sound of bat hitting ball filled the air once more, as the baseball soared high into the blue sky. Another homer!

The crowd was on the edge of its seats now, witnessing a rare exhibition of power-hitting prowess in the game. But Ty Cobb wasn't done yet. He approached the plate for the third time that afternoon, his confidence skyrocketing. Perhaps scared in the presence of such a powerful hitter, the St. Louis pitcher sent the fastball hurtling towards home plate.

Nonetheless, Cobb's gaze remained fixed on the ball, his muscles coiled like a spring ready for action. Crack! The third home run of the day flew over the outfield fence, as the stadium erupted into a thunderous roar.

Ty Cobb had accomplished the seemingly impossible with three home runs in three at-bats, a feat reserved for baseball legends. Even the fans of the opposing side applauded the stunning display of strength and precision from the man they had so frequently despised as a rival.

As the game came to a close, the Tigers won thanks to Ty Cobb's extraordinary performance. That day, Ty Cobb's legend grew even more. He had hushed the critics, astounded the fans, and made an unforgettable stamp on baseball history.

For years to come, that game would be remembered in whispers as one of the most remarkable displays of power hitting ever seen on a baseball diamond. Ty Cobb's three-home run game on that amazing day in 1925 would forever establish his legacy as one of baseball's best players.

Chapter 29
The Four Homers that Made History – Mike Schmidt

The baseball world assembled at Wrigley Field in the spring of 1976, anticipating a match between the Philadelphia Phillies and the Chicago Cubs. They had no idea that this would be a day engraved into the books of baseball history, a day when one man would stand above the rest, leaving an everlasting stamp on the sport.

Mike Schmidt, the Phillies' outstanding third baseman, was the center of attention on that day. At the first crack of the bat, something amazing was about to happen.

Mike Schmidt, full name Michael Jack Schmidt, was born on September 27, 1949, in Dayton, Ohio, USA. He is a retired professional baseball player widely considered as one of the greatest third basemen in Major League history.

Schmidt attended Ohio University, where he excelled in both baseball and basketball. The Philadelphia Phillies selected him as the second overall choice in the 1971 MLB Draft. Schmidt made his Major League Baseball debut with the Philadelphia Phillies on September 12, 1972.

His outstanding offensive and defensive performances made him a fan favorite and gained him the respect of players and fans across the league. Schmidt's leadership and passion to the game earned him the title of Phillies captain, establishing his status as a club icon.

Throughout his illustrious baseball career, Mike Schmidt faced numerous challenges that tested his ability and mental fortitude. Schmidt struggled in the early parts of his Major League career to adjust to the increased competition, dealing with issues involving consistency at the plate and defensive effectiveness at third base. Rather than giving up, he used his early setbacks to polish his skills and refine his strategy on both offense and defense. Schmidt endured enormous pressure and tremendous expectations as a top player for the Philadelphia Phillies from both the fans and the media. Nonetheless, he transformed this pressure into motivation, pushing himself to rise to the occasion at crucial moments and deliver stellar performances.

Schmidt worked hard to avoid sacrificing one aspect of his game for the other, striving to strike a balance between his offensive prowess as a power hitter and his devotion to brilliance on the defensive end. His unwavering work ethic, self-awareness, and commitment to learning and growth cemented his place as one of baseball's most well-rounded players.

On April 17, 1976, Mike Schmidt played in one of the most famous and iconic games of his career against the Philadelphia Phillies at Wrigley Field.

Schmidt entered the batter's box at the top of the first inning, with runners on base. He squared off against the Cubs' pitcher, his gaze fixed on the ball with unwavering purpose. The crack of his bat echoed throughout the stadium as he launched the baseball into the upper atmosphere. His three-run home run set the tone for the rest of the game.

But that was just the start of the spectacle. Schmidt returned to the plate in the second inning, the taste of victory still in the air. As the ball met his bat with an authoritative crack, Schmidt sent another home run into the stands. With each swing, this baseball monster made history-- the Cubs and their fans could only watch in wonder.

The game continued, and Schmidt's fame increased with each at-bat. He came up big again in the fourth inning, defying the odds with another home run. The stunned audience held its breath, thinking they were watching a once-in-a-lifetime event.

Schmidt appeared unstoppable as the game progressed into the later innings. His tremendous swings and unrivaled concentration drove the ball over the fence for the fourth time. Only a few people in baseball history have hit four home runs in a single game. The stadium exploded in a symphony of cheers and acclaim, giving tribute to a man who had stepped into greatness.

The final out was made, and the Phillies won, but it was Mike Schmidt who had conquered the day. He'd etched his name into the record books, alongside the game's immortals. The baseball world was in awe of the man who had accomplished the virtually impossible by transforming Wrigley Field into his own triumph playground.

Chapter 30
A Strikeout King – Randy Johnson

T he Arizona Diamondbacks and the San Diego Padres were getting ready for a big game at Bank One Ballpark on a steamy June evening in 2004. On that very same evening, Randy Johnson, a fearsome left-handed pitcher known as "The Big Unit," was on the verge of writing himself into baseball history.

On September 10, 1963, Randall David Johnson was born in Walnut Creek, California. He would grow to be considered one of the most dominant baseball pitchers in Major League baseball. After four years at USC, Johnson was taken by the Montreal Expos in the second round of the 1985 Major League Baseball Draft.

Johnson was known for his blistering fastball, lethal slider, and commanding presence on the mound. His fastball frequently reached velocities of more than 100 mph, making him one of the most feared pitchers in baseball. His power pitching combined with his frightening height made him a terror for opposing batters.

Randy Johnson faced and overcame numerous challenges over his incredible baseball career, shaping him into one of the game's most formidable pitchers. Due to his imposing height and long limbs, Johnson struggled with control and command early on, but he worked relentlessly on refining his mechanics and delivery to develop better control over his pitches. When he made his Major League debut, he faced the challenge of adjusting to higher competition levels, but he exploited this adjustment to improve his pitch selection and mental game. To handle the demands of an MLB season, his towering frame necessitated great physical endurance, prompting him to prioritize conditioning and fitness.

Having suffered injuries at various periods in his career, he utilized these obstacles to heal and strengthen his physique in order to avoid future setbacks. Johnson took advantage of the possibilities that came with migrating to new teams, learning from different coaching staff and teammates, which enriched his game. Furthermore, when confronted with increased expectations from fans and the media, he redirected them into inspiration, propelling him to exceed the lofty goals he set for himself. Johnson's persistent devotion to learning, adaptability, mental resilience, and passion to the game helped shape him into one of the most dominant pitchers in Major League baseball.

On June 29, 2004, in a game against the San Diego Padres at Bank One Ballpark in Phoenix, Arizona, Randy Johnson recorded his 4,000th career strikeout.

It was clear from the first pitch that Johnson was at the top of his game. His slider raced out of the strike zone and his fastball sizzled, leaving Padres hitters swinging in vain. The crowd's anticipation for Johnson's historic 4,000th career strikeout grew with each successive out.

With a runner on first base and two outs in the second inning, Johnson got his chance to shine. The Padres' Jeff Cirillo swung and missed at his dazzling slider. As the umpire clearly indicated strike three, the crowd exploded. The scoreboard announced Randy Johnson's achievement: he had thrown his 4,000th career strikeout.

The game was put on hold momentarily as a tribute to the left-handed player. The fans in Arizona gave Johnson a standing ovation, recognizing his greatness as a baseball player and a historical figure.

Despite the Diamondbacks' eventual loss that night to the Padres, the game will live on in baseball history. Randy Johnson's remarkable talent and dominance as a pitcher were on full display, making this an unforgettable moment in his legendary career. Reaching 4,000 strikeouts in his career cemented his place as one of baseball's all-time greats in that arena.

Baseball fans all across the world will always remember Randy Johnson's historic milestone game as a special occasion to honor the career of "The Big Unit" and his place in baseball fame.

Conclusion

As we leave the field of baseball history, we find ourselves surrounded by countless great players who have made an unforgettable impression on the game and on our hearts. These baseball legends have not only amazed us with their spectacular on-field heroics, but also taught us valuable lessons about life. Everyone, including these legendary athletes, has to face challenges and setbacks in life.

Their experiences inspire us to keep going when the going gets rough, because no matter how bad things go, we can overcome anything if we put our minds to it. The ability to bounce back from setbacks and improve with every swing of the bat and throw of the ball is represented by this mental toughness.

It's important to keep in mind that success is not just measured in home runs and wins, but in the refusal to give up on oneself or one's goals. In the immortal words of Babe Ruth: "Never let the fear of striking out keep you from playing the game." The desire to take chances and to try our best despite the odds being stacked against us is what ultimately leads to success.

Baseball has shown us that there is still something to gain from adversity. The lessons we learn from failure—whether it's a strikeout, dropped ball, or loss—can help us become better players and people in the future.

Let the lives of these baseball greats serve as an inspiration to you, young readers, as you set out on your own paths in life. Accept the challenges, rejoice in the successes, and value the journey toward your own goals!

Made in the USA
Las Vegas, NV
14 September 2023